CONTENTS

Face your shadow, lead your life

YOU
ARE
THE
ONE

PINE G. LAND

*"For the world,
the known and the unknown."*

Big appreciation to my husband Alberto and my son Mango for being patient with me.

YOU ARE THE ONE

By

PINE G. LAND

AUTHOR'S NOTE

No matter what you read or see or hear, there will always be something that goes against your comfortable emotional/mental state. Some of the information in this book will challenge your old paradigms/beliefs.

There are as many truths as there are people. All the billions of little truths make the absolute WHOLE ONE. I don't really use social media anymore. Whenever I was using them daily, I was posting book pages from many different authors. Quite often, some people would reply with:

"You don't find truths in books".

These were people that had spiritual ego, thinking that they were above others. Those people (the ones that said "You don't find truths in books"), don't realize they know nothing compared to the intelligent higher beings that are above everyone, in knowledge and understanding. We too are intelligent when we are our true selves. To arrive at a point where you will find the absolute knowledge/truth from within, you will have to research articles, videoclips and of course books.

Many author's thoughts on books come from their own mind, so why not put those thoughts into writing for others to read? The point is that truth is scattered everywhere, truth is found in all books, including the religious ones. But any information is just that, information. Something is true when it resonates from within. Different people express themselves in their own way, different words are perceived differently from different people. Whatever you read here, question from within, use your rational mind, but also be careful because the rational mind rationalizes based on memories and personal experiences.

The more points of view that you consider as a sliver of truth, the bigger the angle that you can view the truth from. Never reject information that doesn't align with your beliefs. Just put it aside for the moment, one day what you previously thought was nonsense, might prove to be useful in the development of your character and personality.

As you might have already noticed, English is not my mother language. I was born and raised in Austria, I lived in Canada for 5 years and then I moved to the U.S.A. But I was already speaking English before that. The grammar will never be perfect, I hope you get past that. The message and the intention are more important.

While reading this book, have these three points in mind:

1... The author was born and raised in a non-English speaking country.

2... Do no believe anything in this book unless the information resonates with you, and even then, question yourself on a regular basis because resonating is not always positive. For example, two people that like to gossip or love to watch horror movies, these people resonate with each other. They're simply on the same/similar low frequency field/scale.

3... See this book (or any other book) as fiction, this way you will not get disappointed by expectation. Consequently, you will get rewarded, meaning that you will learn a thing or two since you shouldn't expect any external information to satisfy your beliefs that you acquired over a lifetime of external conditioning.

You may encounter certain words that may be spelt differently then what you are accustomed to, because of regional differences such as American, Canadian or British English.

ALWAYS CONSIDER EVIDENCE
THAT CONTRADICTS YOUR BELIEFS.

THINK FOR YOURSELF

1 I follow one rule when I read any book. I treat any book as a fictional read. This way I have zero disappointments. My suggestion to you when you read books, is to pay attention to things that resonate and things that don't. What resonates, doesn't mean that it is true, and what does not resonate, doesn't mean it is a lie. What a lie is and what a truth is, has simply to do with what you believe yourself to be, what you believe the world to be. Your beliefs dictate moral relativism.

The absolute truth is within yourself, in your DNA and not in yours or anyone else's opinions about anything. Just as what I am writing is (should be) just an opinion from your perspective. It is perfectly fine to read/hear other people's opinion because words are powerful. Words can trigger discernment. The only truth is what you personally experience. Have you ever stopped and thought about how magical you are? Just the fact that you are capable of breathing, is magic in itself.

COLLATERAL TEACHING
Ever heard of "collateral damage?" We will talk about the opposite of this. This is about helping as opposed to damaging someone. An example of how to teach someone without even talking to them is to do things in their presence. If you have a child that needs to lose weight, then you walk every day in the house, run, go up and down the stairs. If you do this many days, a seed will be planted in his mind. Depending on how strong they are, they may water the seed while they are with you, or at a later time. Just try to remember how many things you do or don't do because of repetitions from your parents that you had to go through when you were a child or as a young adult.

Governments or corporations are not your friend, we are just digital numbers in their eyes, you are something to be used and disposed of. The government is also a corporation, so is the Name and the LAST NAME on your legal documents. For more on this, check at the end of the book (Resources) for the names of two books that talk about this subject "the STRAWMAN".

DO NOT DONATE, STARVE THE BEAST
For a long time, there have been many donation or charity organizations. Even though I have no doubt that some have been genuine from people that care about humanity, most of them existed/exist for personal gain. What is worse is when people donate body parts such as hair, skin, semen etc.

Hair contains your DNA. Do not donate it anywhere. Any donations of your body parts/substances that you make must remain in your possession. The government does not have your best interest in mind. You don't want to be cloned do you? The same applies to when people donate sperm, or blood or anything. With the exception of when you have to donate blood to your children when they need it. Otherwise, do not donate any part of you. You were given your body (and everything else it contains) so that you could remain complete and not be diminished, dimmed out or completely eradicated. This mindset that I have, is based on understanding the beast. The beast is the system that thrives on people's suffering.

WHY CAN'T I (most people) LET GO OF WHO HAS DONE ME WRONG IN THE PAST?
Any wrongdoing from co-workers, siblings, lovers of the past are a result of versions of people that do not exist anymore. It is madness to engage emotionally in the present for something that happened in the past. When you hold onto a grudge, you create a bad version of that person that has done you wrong or that you think that has wronged you in the past. Many people create stories in their mind about how someone hurt them. Although sometimes others may have indeed hurt you physically, the hurt in your mind/feelings is on you for allowing them to penetrate your fortress intentionally or unintentionally.

Your feelings are yours and yours alone, nobody can hurt them, only you can. Then you end up blaming others for your weakness. I speak from experience. All of us want to live in peace and be happy, all of us try our best to survive but is life really about just surviving or living it? Survival mode makes you harsh toward others, either in a mean way or in a fake way by being nice using sweet words that don't come from an open heart but from a poisoned mind. To live your life, universal insight/guidelines must be followed/respected.

CRUCIAL LIFE GUIDELINES

1.When you are angry, mind your ***TEMPER.***
2.When you are alone, mind your ***THOUGHTS.***
3.When you are in trouble, mind your ***EMOTIONS.***
4.When you are with friends, mind your ***TONGUE.***
5.When you are with a group, mind your ***BEHAVIOR.***
6.When the Universe starts blessing you, mind your ***EGO.***

1.When you are angry, mind your ***TEMPER.***

Anger is trapped emotions, it is trapped unresolved trauma. A lot of trauma is buried and suppressed within most people. Most people refuse to deal with them. Healing cannot happen on a deeper level unless the past trauma is dealt with. You have to face your own shadow. The longer you resist, the harder it will be for you to face the monster within that you created. Go out in the Sun and try to run away from your shadow. Do you think you can escape it? You can't run from what is a part of you, you can only face that illusion and tame it. You have the power to make your shadow work for you, empower you and help you climb higher in the ladder of self-awareness steps.

2.When you are alone, mind your ***THOUGHTS.***

Let us begin with a fact. Anything that you are thinking at any given time comes from the spiritual realm or the non-physical dimension. Your brain is a tool, a transmitter. Think of your brain as a TV channel. Your thoughts are countless number of TV channels. You do not know the source of the channels' information. You can only see or hear the information through the screen. You have the power to change any TV channel that you desire. You are in full power, you are the remote control.

At times, you will have periods of down time where your central system a.k.a. your brain needs to recharge. Meditation recharges your brain. Meditation doesn't always have to be in a living room with your eyes closed. Meditation can be experienced everywhere when you engage with love and genuine intention on virtually everything that you engage in life.

Gardening is a form of meditation. Speaking of gardening, when you plant flowers or vegetables or fruit trees, you are creating an ecosystem for bugs, worms, butterflies etc. The butterflies will fly away if you keep chasing them. But if you build and work on a beautiful garden, the butterflies will come to you. **See the garden as your mind and the butterflies as your thoughts.** If you focus on improving yourself, anything that you desire will come to you effortlessly. You attract what you are.

3.When you are in trouble, mind your *EMOTIONS*.

Have you ever met someone that never had any negative emotions such as anger or worry or fear? I don't think so. Even if you actually met someone without any of these emotions, it doesn't mean that they never experienced those emotions when they were not in your presence. Know that negative (or positive) emotions can be internal, without the person expressing it externally. That is even more dangerous when you keep emotional distress inside you. When you keep suppressed emotions inside of you long enough, disease will begin to manifest.

Suppressed emotions are suppressed energy/frequency. Energy is meant to always flow and not to be enslaved. Eventually, the suppressed energy will explode in the form of a disease within your organs. Think twice before reacting to someone. Breathing deep and consciously ensures that oxygen travels fast in the front part of your brain where the thinking part of the brain is. This way you will not rush and explode emotionally.

4.When you are with friends, mind your *TONGUE*.

We humans are gossipers. We are trained to not mind our own business. We are trained to communicate with the outside world and to ignore the inner one. The real world/reality is in your mind, that's where you came from and that's where you will go after your last breath. While you are alive, mind your tongue. There is a saying that says, *"Your tongue doesn't have any bones but it can break bones"*. Which means that your words may seem innocent but they can destroy someone if you speak without first thinking thoroughly.

Everyone in your life has already formed a specific version of you in their heads. Only you know who you truly are so when you express yourself to others, not everyone will understand what you mean. Even if they do, in their head they will elaborate the information even further according to their own point of view. Consequently, according to their new version of what you previously said, they will reply/think to another version of you that they created according to what you said to them. It is like a snowball effect.

So, mind your tongue, speak little and with clarity. Even then, people will still misunderstand you. How they filter your words is not your concern. Your concern is to think twice and speak with genuine intention. If people still have a problem with what you say, then move onto other people that may put the effort in understanding you.

5.When you are with a group, mind your **BEHAVIOR.**

What you think, is the seed of your behavior. Thoughts breed words and emotions which then manifest as behavior. What you think of yourself and others will determine your behavior. In order to spread happiness in the presence of a person or a group, mind your behavior. Everyone else won't have to cater to your immediate needs and vice versa. Be willing to listen to other people's opinion without having to accept them as your reality. Their words is their reality just as your words are your reality. If you want change in your life, remember this process: **thoughts> words> emotions> behavior.**

6.When the Universe starts blessing you, mind your **EGO.**

Ego is your lower self, your animalistic nature. The *'Ego'* feels threatened anytime you get out of your comfort zone. We have been played by the black magicians (this realm's controllers). We have to have a total ego breakdown of all we thought we knew and we must be willing to surrender to the fact that reality was never what we believed it to be.

Not many people have the courage to turn their life around, most people would rather keep sleeping, even though it seems that more people are awakened than before. At one point or another in life, the universe blesses you with riches in the form or money, land, or people. Do not take things for granted. We value something when we lose it, we don't appreciate the blessings when we have them. Just being alive at this time is a blessing in itself.

YOUR SPIRIT CANNOT BE KILLED, BUT IT CAN BE ENSLAVED

Some people fail to understand something very important when it is about the difference between a spirit and the physical body. There is no difference aside from the appearance (physical) and non appearance (spirit). Physical and non-physical bodies are sides of the same coin. They are two different frequencies in one. One cannot exist without the other in the grand scheme of things. Each individual being's spirit is eternal, it can never be destroyed. The spirit, or energy can only be transformed, it can only change form.

Any kind of energy can be manipulated for good or for bad, depending on who is doing the manipulation. Are you manipulating your own energy or are you allowing others to cause changes in you based on their personal intentions? Some people say: "I don't care about this or about that, I am eternal, I'll never die". These people have heard or read that the energy (in this case the 'spirit') can never be destroyed and they are failing to understand that their physical body is the coat (clothing) of their spirit. If you abuse your physical body with alcohol, processed foods/drinks, porn, negative thinking/behavior etc., you are enslaving yourself therefore you are enslaving your spirit. Unfortunately, the spoken/written language is limited.

When I say "your spirit", it sounds as if the spirit is separated from you, as if the spirit is outside of you or something that you possess. This is inaccurate. Your spirit and your physical, emotional and mental bodies are ONE. It is very important to understand that anything bad that you inflict on yourself whether it be physically, mentally and/or emotionally, you are causing harm to your spirit, meaning "YOU".

HAPPY EVERYDAY AND NOT HAPPY HOLYDAY

When are you alive? Every day? Or on specific days of the year? People have been conditioned to be supposedly happy when the government tells them to. Every year, before a so-called holiday, people think or talk about it so they plant the seed of destruction in them. Every moment that you breathe, you are alive. Yesterday was the previous **present moment** and tomorrow will be the next **present moment**. Tomorrow or next month or next year have not arrived yet. When they arrive, it will be another 'today'. Technically, the past and the future do not exist. Yes, you have memories from the so-called past, but you are not the same person you were a year ago, 6 months ago or yesterday. With every new thought you are a new person. If you think you are the same person, then you associate yourself with an illusion which is your name, your job, your ideologies, your social status etc. Think for yourself, don't hang around with people just because it is difficult to be by yourself.

Try and be by yourself in a room for a few hours without tv, cellphone or anything to keep you distracted. That's when you'll know how awakened you are. That's when you will deal with the real darkness, the one within your mind which suppressed the light from shining. You and only you decide to transmute darkness into light. Associating yourself with your age/numbers will contribute to your degeneration of your physical body. See days or any event as joyful moments in the unlimited stream of time.

We are created to create. We are creators. We are not created to live a passive, uninteresting and mundane life. If you feel bored in anyway, know that's the moment you have lost the purpose of life. Create daily and watch your life become a blissful experience.

> EVERY MOMENT YOU ARE A DECISION
> AWAY FROM TOTALLY CHANGING YOUR LIFE.

I THINK THEREFORE I AM

*"The only thing we have power over in
the universe, is our own thoughts"* - Rene Descartes

2 The Devil (those that want you to be a slave) can only trick you through the 5-sense reality, but what they cannot trick, is your pineal gland when it is fully opened. Your third eye/pineal gland is the 6th sense. The PRIDE flag has only 6 colors/colours as opposed to 7. They omitted one colour, indigo which represents the pineal gland/3rd eye chakra. Not only that, but the colours of the flag are inverted, to keep you stuck/attached/enslaved to the root, sacral and solar plexus energy centers. They don't what you to go beyond/above the bottom three chakras or energetic centers. "Colors" are how light/information enter inside you. Your body, mind and the soul needs the colours in the right order, in order for you to be functioning in harmony with the divine.

Colours play a huge part in enslaving or freeing people. Many times online, I have seen people that claim to be awakened and yet, when they comment online, many of them comment the 6 colour undivine flag or emoji. There are no flags with 7 colours (emojis or anything posted/advertised by the mainstream dark forces/power) online because all social media are controlled by THEM. Everything begins and ends in the GREAT MIND. Your mind is simply a grain of sand, part of the WHOLE. Rene Descartes had a great idea/explanation on how to know what is true. Are our senses deceiving us? Think of something that you know is definitely true. How can you be sure that is true?

These kinds of questions troubled the 17th-century Christian philosopher Rene Descartes. How can we be sure that anything that we *think* is real and true actually *is* real and true and not an illusion? To resolve this problem, he decided that he would doubt everything that he believed; he would then see whether there was anything left at the end that he could know for certain. If he could not be 100% certain about a certain belief, then his test would fail. Descartes decided that he could no longer trust his senses to tell him what is true because sometimes our senses give us false information. For example, when you look through the binoculars from the other end, or a spoon or object in a glass of water which would seem like it's bent, but that's not true, that's simply an illusion, meaning our eyes are deceiving us. Sometimes our hearing deceives us, we think we hear something but in fact we don't. Descartes ruled out the possibility of knowing anything for certain through the use of the 5 senses.

Are our minds being tricked?

Descartes ruled out knowing anything for certain through using the rational mind (reason), for example mathematical truths such as 2+2=4. He thought that he could not prove that there is not an evil demon tricking us into thinking 2+2=4 every time we do the sum when actually 2+2=5! Descartes was troubled by the fact that everything his mind thought was real and true could be an illusion. He could be nothing more then a mind trapped in an evil demon's laboratory. If this were the case, Descartes wondered, what one thing could the demon *not* trick his mind about?

Descartes realized that the demon would not be able to trick his mind into thinking it existed if it did not. In order for the demon to trick his mind, he would have to have a mind. He summed up this idea by writing one of the best-known lines in all of philosophy: '**I think, therefore I am.**'

Descartes thought that the fact he could not doubt his own existence meant he must exist. He did not think this proved he had a body; the demon could be tricking him into thinking he had a body. However, he must have a thinking mind; otherwise, there would be nothing for the demon to trick. Descartes did not think that this could prove that anybody else existed; these could still be illusions. It wouldn't work for him to say, '*You think, therefore you are*' or '*We think, therefore we are*', but he could be certain of his own existence. This is sometimes called the *first certainty* and is often written in Latin, ***cogito ergo sum*** which when translated into English, means '*I think, therefore I am.*' When you think for yourself, then you truly know your existence.

YOU ARE THE CENTER OF THE UNIVERSE

The whole universe works for you, you projected it from your own mind. Every second of your life that you live in, is the present moment, the center of everything that is in your mind. Therefore, you are in the center of your universe. Just as I am the center of my universe. From your point of existence to you I am an NPC (non-playable character). Just as you are an NPC to me. You have never met me in person, you do not know what I look like and you have no idea what's in the depth of my mind. The same applies if we reverse the roles. I don't know you. But even if we were siblings, it would still apply just the same.

The only person that you will ever know, is YOU. "I think therefore I am" is valid when you think for yourself. If you are thinking about watching sports {sports are distractions}, or buying jewelleries/materialistic things {that's consumerism}, or if you watch porn or are ruled by sexual urges {that's the wrong way to use the creative sexual energy}, all of these distractions are not "*thinking for yourself*", these are implants, viruses that keeps your highest potential hidden from you. If you have questions about your existence, then you are on the right track. The next question should be that of wanting to know who you are.

There are only 24h in a day/night cycle. How much time do you spend at work, at parties, gossiping, shopping, with your family, children etc.? How much time is left to spend talking to yourself? Not much, I reckon. Practice solitude so that you are met face to face (metaphorically) with your real self, the invisible one, the great mind that is in the center of your brain, your pineal gland. To have a fully opened third eye you must lose your human mind, or else you will not gain your spiritual senses and you will not be able to grow spiritually.

When you relinquish the confines of the human mind, there comes a pivotal moment, you begin to embrace the expansive spiritual realm found within yourself awaiting for you to give it wings. The wings won't open unless you shed the illusions. Eventually, the wings will take you to heights you never imagined possible before. You will fly to the boundless vistas of inner truths of higher consciousness.

> DO YOU THINK OR DO YOU
> THINK YOU THINK?

KARMA = ACTION

3 Unfortunately, the word 'karma' is used by most people to describe a bad, negative action/situation.

For every action there is an equal reaction which means **CAUSE and EFFECT**

Good Karma = Good deeds bring rewards. Anything you do to improve your life without taking anyone else's freedom away, will come back to you in the form of rewards, or blessings if you want to use that term. The Intelligent Design, or the Universe will function as intended, regardless if your actions are intentional or not. That is why it is very important to be a self-aware person where you make conscious moral choices so that the universe works for you and not against. What is your purpose in life? Your purpose gets fulfilled when you give love to yourself and everything in the world. Little things you say or do make a big difference in the outcome of your life's journey. When you take a bit of time and dedicate it to:

- *Talk to someone that needs help.*

- *When you saved that cat in the traffic.*

- *When you let someone in a rush ahead of you in line at the grocery store.*

- *When you helped that old lady crossed the road.*

- *When you helped you mother or anyone else for that matter no matter how little effort you put, if it was from you heart, you fulfil*led your purpose. You shone some light in the dark path ahead.

If you equate your purpose with goal-based achievements you end up unhappy, you end up awaiting for the next dopamine (illusion/ destination). The mind can always deceive you but not your heart. Do good and forget, do bad and regret. If you genuinely help someone from your heart, you don't expect anything in return, therefore you forget, the universe will take care of it, you will be rewarded. If you expect something in return, then what you did was not from your heart, you were deceived by your mind, more precisely your lower mind.

Bad Karma=Bad deeds bring punishment, debts to be paid. You must pay for infringing the universal law that says to allow all sentient beings to be free. You don't owe the debt to anyone else but yourself. Your own actions can be poisons or remedies.

That's what karma means - **ACTION-REACTION**. You reap what you sow.

Just today I had a situation with a friend of mine about the **cause-and-effect** subject. Me and him went to grocery shopping, when we returned home, he parked the front of the car by his house's entrance. He got mad, because he should have parked the other way, so we didn't have to do unnecessary trips to the back of his car to pick up the stuff that he bought. He blamed me for his mistake, he said that I was distracting him with talking about something (the subject doesn't matter). I was like:

```
"You did this to yourself, you caused this, and the
effect came back to you. If you stop blaming other
people, you will have a clear mind and make the
right choices where the outcome/effect becomes a
reward/comfort rather then discomfort/punishment."
```

This is just a simple example that doesn't harm, but when you are not a clear minded person you can make mistakes that can cause you and others to suffer or even die as a result of the universal law of CAUSE and EFFECT. Death serves to remind you to live, but have people realized that? Reincarnation is simply the effect of the cause. If you don't want to reincarnate again, then you must purify yourself. You must purify your body, emotions, thoughts and your spirit. There are no shortcuts in real life.

Shortcuts happen only in the man-made illusion. Simply analyze your life as to why you are happy or unhappy. You can't blame your parents or the government or any other person or thing. That's you and only you creating the cause (*action*) and the effect (*reaction*). Anyone else is a player in this game called life. In your game you are the main character, you are the one that dictates the circumstances and not the other way around. If the circumstances dictate your life, then you give the power of free will to others to do with your life as they please. Nonetheless, it was you that was the cause of that effect.

The same applies when life blesses you. You are still the cause and the blessings are the effect. There is no higher power to reward or punish you. You are the higher power. If you refuse to believe that you are the highest power in your life, then you will keep causing a chain reaction of events that will benefit others and not you.

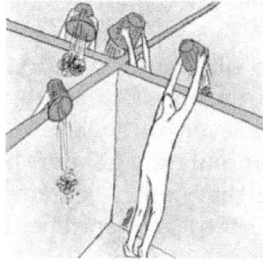

Everything you do will come back to you. Nobody can escape this, this is a universal law. You punish yourself if you have selfish intentions or you reward yourself if your intentions come from the heart. The punishment can come at different times in life and in all forms. If you do something bad, something may happen to you or perhaps to your child or your parents where you'll now have to take care of them, meaning giving your life/freedom for the greater good, a.k.a. helping someone else in need. The universe (use the word God if you wish) listens to your wishes and desires.

The more potent your intention is towards something, the more the universe will create the circumstances to serve you. A temporary positive negative punishment is "money". You could make a lot of money and collect a big amount of riches and you might say that you hurt and deceived people and you still got rewarded. When you have a lot of money, you have a little heart or none at all. Without a heart you are a robot, a piece of rock. Is that a life that you want where everyone you know would use you for money as opposed to for your personality/character? Now, I don't mean that it is better to be poor than rich.

The same way the hypothetical situation of a bad person that became rich by exercising (knowingly or unknowingly to him) the law of manifestation/cause and effect, the same way it works for when you want to have prosperity when you use the same law the hypothetical bad man used. If you hang out with people that lie, deceive, gossip etc., you will inflict bad karma on yourself because the frequency of those people will affect you. The opposite is equally true if you hang around with people that are honest, loving and caring, thinking for themselves and are striving to create a better world. Choose wisely who you hang around with.

I had situations where some people I know who don't hang around with a lot of people but still feel sad, anxious, worried etc. Why is that? Because these people spend too much time on social media reading and commenting on all kinds of posts where people spill their drama. The low frequency energy coming from a real person in real life is no different than a random stranger online. Energy doesn't care about people, animals, technology etc. Energy is neutral, energy goes whenever you send it. You wield the sword, you are an alchemist, you manipulate the energy however you wish. Most people struggle because they inflict bad karma on themselves not knowing the importance of the universal law **cause and effect** .

THROW A STONE ABOVE YOUR HEAD IN THE AIR. WILL THE
STONE STAY IN THE AIR OR FALL ON YOU?

DON'T DIMINISH YOURSELF BY GIVING OTHERS' WORDS MORE POWER THAN YOUR OWN.

4 Words are powerful, you can empower or destroy yourself by them, even if your intention is genuine. One example is:

'I don't know what I would have done without you'

It is true that anyone can help you when you are in need, whether it is an intentional or collateral/unintentional help. It is enough by saying "Thank you, I appreciate what you did for me". Mean it from your heart. When you say, *'I don't know what I would have done without you'* you are now diminishing yourself. You are telling yourself that you are not enough, that you cannot overcome darkness without someone else's help. The outside world exists only in your head. What you think of anything or anyone, is only in your head, a projection from within.

All your expressions are based on who you truly are in the moment. You become what you say. If what you say is who you are, then how come you become someone else as a result of being affected by external words/opinions? Those are injections of words/phrases from the outside world. The injections can be remedies or cures, depending on who said it, someone that empowers you, someone that wants to harm you, or none of the above, perhaps it is you that harms yourself by not knowing how powerful you are so you allow external conditioning to affect you in a diminishing way. Think twice before doing something, don't act on impulses. Knowing who you truly are and having an idea or who you are, is not the same thing.

Whatever it is that you do, do it with love from your heart. Of course, you should think for yourself, but do not let chaos determine your behavior. Anyone may be strong when they are by themselves, but you are the strongest in the middle of chaos and how you deal with it. Always take deep breaths when situations arise where you could be triggered to act without thinking. When you consciously take deep breaths, then you are in the moment. When you are in the moment, the past and the future do not exist therefore, you will not be driven to scream, be worried or anxious from memories of bad experiences of the past or worries/anxiety of future events that have not happened yet.

Just as anything external is a projection from within your mind, you are a projection in other people's minds, a version of you of course. The real version of you is only in you. Why give other people's words more power than your own when what they think of you is just a creation in their own mind? I'm strictly speaking about people that want to harm you or that have something to gain from you which causes them to use your weak points by forcing you to have irrational thoughts and behavior.

When you speak without thinking for yourself, you are like an open book to people, you are allowing them to bring their guns in the flowery field that you live. The point is that you have to help people when you can but also must think because not everyone has your best interest in their mind. They will take advantage of you, they will take from you as much as you allow yourself to give.

THIS IS A DARK ROOM
Even though light goes through your eyes for these words to be read by you, you are still in a dark room. This (or any other book) is like a dark room where the light is so dim that you cannot see it unless you step back for a moment so that your focus improves. This book is like being in the middle of the ocean at night and yet you are surrounded by unlimited light sources. One light is my intention of writing this book, another source of light is the interpretation you have of certain words.

As an example, in the previous chapter Karma=Action, I deliberately explained/mentioned both "good and bad karma" terms because most people have been conditioned to only use the word karma in a negative way. Now you know there is good and bad karma, which means good and bad deeds. These cause reactions in the form of punishments or rewards. Having this knowledge/understanding, is like seeing the light in the middle of the darkness. When you understand and are conscious of how you express yourself, you speak with confidence and are not manipulated or affected by other people's words.

Another light source in the middle of the darkness is the books by other authors mentioned in this book. If I didnt mention any other authors' books, it would be like hitting a wall. Since I mention other authors in this book, now you have different light sources. Since different authors express themselves differently, now you have the opportunity to be exposed to more knowledge and point of views. Otherwise you'd be left out only with my thoughts. Obviously, I am providing my thoughts (a path) and the direction of other paths (other books mentioned here) which all paths will eventually converge and lead you to the main path.

No matter how much you think you know and understand, there will always be authors (other books) that will give you some kind of further insight. See my thoughts and other people's thoughts as cooking ingredients. You are the cook or the alchemist or the builder of your life's journey, you decide how to build a strong foundation before adding floors to your creation.

My thoughts and other people's thoughts are available for you too, in the aether. Just as what you think daily can be accessed be me and others (only if the psychic ability is really developed). There have been many documented cases where different inventors from different areas of the world invented the same thing. Technically, they didn't invent anything, they just rediscovered what was already in the Book Of Life or in the Akashic Records as it is known by many in the spiritual community. You can develop the same ability. The ingredients that makes us magical are already in us. It's all about determination, will and discipline and we can accomplish anything.

> YOU ARE AS LOW OR AS HIGH AS YOU THINK
> YOU ARE. YOUR WORDS CAN CUT OR HEAL
> YOU.

NAMES DON'T MATTER, THE MESSAGE DOES

5 Countless of people are stuck on names, they worship names to the point that if some information doesn't come from said name, then it is not worth it to know. An example is the word "God". This word doesn't sit right with some but it does with others. Last year, on Facebook I posted a page from a book called '*I AM THE KEY THAT OPENS ALL DOORS*' by Saimir Kercanaj. The title of the chapter is 'WHAT OR WHO IS GOD?'. Below an excerpt from that chapter that some people had a problem with, especially with the part where it says that "God is not a creator":

> "God is consciousness, **not a creator** (as in a physical man up in the sky). Although I have used a few times the word "God" here and in my other books, but when I use it, it's to describe the Supreme Creator/Consciousness so don't get hung up on the word. God is the source of creation itself. "IT" (not he or she). IT is not independent of you. It is the totality of everything. So, when I call myself "GOD" I AM not talking about my personal self. I AM talking about the expression of the God self that rests inside of me, the "I AM", the verb, the ENERGY, not the noun. Once you think God is a noun, person, place or thing, you separate yourself from it and immediately become a limited human being. That's what separates the beLIEvers (organized religion) from the KNOWers (spirituality). Religion has convinced people that God is a person, not only that but it has convinced them that it is a man."

The bolded underlined part in the above excerpt is what triggered some people. These are religious extremists but also non-religious people who grew up in families where the word GOD (a man up in the sky that takes care of everything) was ingrained in their minds. It doesn't matter if you identify yourself as a religious person or not. If you do things because of traditions or because others do it, you might as well call yourself a believer. I, myself in the past have avoided reading books just because I didn't agree with certain words. I was wrong, I missed out on a lot of knowledge and wisdom. I have read all of this author's books. In one of his books (I don't remember which one) he wrote that he finds truth in every book, that every book has something to teach and that the message is what matters and not the name/person. I agree with him 100%.

Another example of how people miss out on knowledge just because they are conditioned to associate truth with certain words, are the words:

- Manifestation.
- Prayer.
- Spells.
- Placebo effect.
- Quantum physics.

In science they use the words QUANTUM PHYSICS
In spirituality they use the word MANIFESTATION
In the Christian belief system they use the word PRAYER
Witches* use the word SPELLS
Atheists call "*manifestation*" PLACEBO EFFECT

Witches - Many people see the word '*witch*' as a bad word, and that is because the church used to burn intelligent spiritual women at the stake. The witches that were getting burned at the stake, were "*white*" witches ("white" as in *benevolent being*, as opposed to dark which means malevolent) women that were trying to balance the world where there would be no more wars, poverty or blood shed. The Church didn't want men to awaken because a society with strong men can never be controlled. Women are designed to lead men into their heart, away from the chaos of the mind. This was inconvenient for the church, since an awakened balanced (feminine/masculine balance) man could never be controlled, so they made laws that prohibited women in position where intelligence was required. This was mostly to suppress men and the women of course but they needed men to become dumb and ready to go to wars and fight for imaginary enemies created by the church and the state. There are white witches and there are dark witches or wizards. There is white and there is dark magic.

In some witches accounts on social media, I have seen amazing posts that are crucial to humanity's awakening. I personally know a couple of people that were avoiding the white witches' accounts just because the word 'witch' was in the usernames of those accounts. The same way I avoided years ago anything that had the word 'prayer'. For years I was using all these terms except the word 'prayer' because I was associating it with religion. I was an ignorant person for not understanding what PRAYER really meant.

The problem with many people that pray or try to manifest good things in life is that they push away what they want by asking (while praying or otherwise) rather than experiencing the feeling as they already have what they want. That's how you manifest the life you want, by imagining your wishes and desires as if you already have what you wish and desire. This way, the universe will bring the circumstances to satisfy your wishes and desires. Some people have a problem with the term 'placebo effect' which is the term science/atheists use. It means the same thing as the other words (manifestation, quantum physics, prayer and spells).

They are all talking about the same thing, the Aether, the unseen, the Supreme intelligent spiritual web/unseen world that holds everything together. Your physical body is a manifestation or a prayer from the Source, the ultimate intelligent seed that manifests anything in the physical world.

God, Creator, Zero-point energy, Supreme intelligence, The ONE , all these terms mean the same thing, they mean the beginning and the end, the Creator. But not as in a person, because if the creator is a man, then it poses the question as to who created the MAN? Some questions are better left alone. People are hurting, lying, deceiving each other on a daily basis. What or Who created us, in the grand scheme of things doesn't matter. The answers will arrive when we learn how to take care of each other instead of how to find more ways to deceive and harm one other.

There is an interesting theory in neuroscience that two different consciousness entities exists inside your mind but only one of them has access to speech. These consciousnesses are God and Satan or higher self or lower self, or the white or the black wolf. You decide whom to feed or serve, God or Satan. For as long as you give your power away to external people, entities or ideologies you will lack in life. The reason is because everything external is a projection from within yourself.

To me you are just a reader, to your father or your mother you are their most precious thing in the world. So, you see, everyone has created a version of you in their head/consciousness. Based on their beliefs, you may be considered a good or a bad person, that is a projection from within their mind. What matters is what you know (not believe to be) to be. You are the one that knows best. When I mean "you" I mean the real divine YOU, not your name. Your name does not matter. Your name is temporary, it was given to you by your parents. What you truly are and what you think to be are two different things.

> WE ARE LITTLE CREATORS. WE CREATE EVERY MOMENT.
> WE CREATE BUT ALSO WE DESTROY. SO. MIND YOUR BEHAVIOR.

BREASTFEEDING CREATES A MORE INTELLIGENT SOCIETY

6 It takes just one generation to improve a civilization's **intelligence**. Mother's milk has the healthiest fat that the baby's brain needs to properly develop. Mother's breast milk contains hormones and the right amount of sugar, protein, fat and all the vitamins necessary to help the baby grow and develop. Breast milk contains antibodies that help protect the baby from many illnesses. Antibodies are protective proteins produced by the immune system in response to foreign substances. But without a strong immune system the antibodies will not be produced as required by intelligent design, so then eventually the baby will become weakened overtime. There is a good reason as to why mother's milk is the best natural/biologic substance for a strong immune system.

I'll add two more things which improve people's **intelligence** further.

1- **Semen retention for men.**
2- **Not wearing any make up, perfumes etc., for women.**

1- Causes men to keep the intelligence within as opposed to wasting it. You'll read later on about this, in chapters *Porn, Semen Retention* etc.
2- Causes women to sense the pheromones of Alpha men. This way, women will be attracted to intelligent men, so when you hang around or get together with emotionally and mentally balanced men, you will be empowered and affected by them. Based on the universal law of "cause and effect", by acting on doing something about anything, you are causing a reaction, a ripple in the universe. For every action there's an equal reaction.

You actions will cause the right men to be magnetized toward you. When you wear make up, perfumes or anything that has a scent, you are covering your own natural scent and you will attract those men that are slaves to their carnal pleasures. Whether you know it or not, if you wear make up, or anything glamourizing (which is fakeness) you are competing with other women for the 'man'. Wearing all that nonsense is like competing so you can win a fast-food burger. There shouldn't be any competition at all. Just be in your natural state as you were designed to be and the right man that is for you will show up from where you won't expect it.

Most men are like children in grown up bodies needing their mother. Since their mother figure is missing (regardless if they grew up with a mother or not) they'll use their partners/wives as a mother needing them to take care of their needs. Men and women have needs that can be fulfilled only by the opposite gender but there must be a limit. When you have your head above your shoulders, your needs will be met willingly by your opposite sex partner as opposed to behaving like a little child that has a fit.

I read a good chapter titled *"Feminization/masculinization of men/women"* page157 in the book titled *GAIN WISDOM THROUGH PRACTICED KNOWLEDGE* by Rimias K. Neo. The author explain the importance of not wearing any perfume or anything that has a scent so that you could attract the right people. Be aware that you can still attract the wrong people, but that is because when you emit light (love and care), parasites (this is not an offence) need to survive so they will be attracted to those of higher frequency. You have nothing to worry about if you think for yourself. You will easily discern between healed or unhealed people. If someone you are interested in is already practicing semen retention, then he is on the right path. Just be careful, some men use this "semen retention" subject to get into your private kingdom.

If you are a man, pay attention to how many social media accounts she has, what people follow her, whom she follows, if she overloads herself with make up, if she goes to clubs etc. then you'll know if she is someone to be with or not. See, different people are at different stages in life, perhaps some people have to go through the darkness. Meaning that someone you are interested in, perhaps they have to go to bars, watch porn, be distracted by news channels, movies, tv shows etc. You can attempt to help someone once, if she/he refuses, then know that this person will drag you down. Think with your brain and not with your genitals.

A lot of women have lost a connection with their motherhood nature. They have been conditioned to believe that health comes from outside/externally. Many parents stuff their children with toys or unhealthy foods to just shut them up because life is so hard that they need some peace which is understandable. But there are things that parents must not give up such as nurturing the root so it can become strong if they want the tree (their children) to thrive.

Many people think their life is hard but if they begin to not consume what makes them think that way, then they would realize that life is not hard. We are hard on ourselves by not thinking for ourselves. Our children pay for our mistakes, laziness and ignorance. You need healing. As I do too. All of us are in the process of healing, some are scratched and some are cut deep. Some just need a band aid and some others need stitches.

> "I hope that in your process of healing, you attract someone who is conscious, deep, passionate, sensitive and spiritual, as much as you are. Someone who makes you believe in yourself and in your self love. Someone who wants to evolve with you, not only in this dimension, but at all levels." Dr. Carl Gustav Jung

YOUR BODY IS THE BEST FACTORY.
MOTHERS: BREASTFEED YOUR CHILDREN WITH
YOUR OWN MILK.

SEXUAL
ENERGY
XCHANGE

THE SECRET COVENANT IS NOT A SECRET ANYMORE

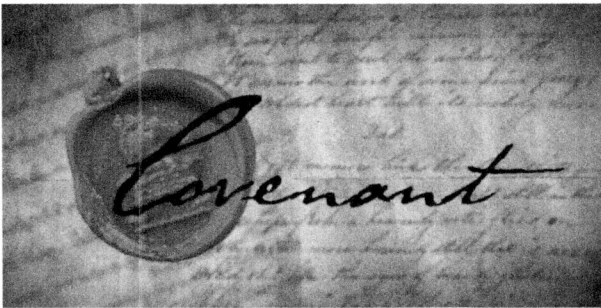

7 You may wonder what this chapter has to do with sexual energy. Well, it has to do with it because through sex many people mate, have children which many of them end up with one parent or with no parents at all. Many marriages/relationships get destroyed as a result of many couples that got artificially tempted to mate and not as a result of real unconditional love. Most marriages and relationships are just business where one or both partners want to gain something out of the other. I was on vacation somewhere in the States (U.S.A.), when I visited a friend's house, checked his library and stumbled across the **Secret Covenant** document in one of the books titled "YOU ARE NOT A STRAWMAN YOU ARE THE ZYGOTE" by Saimir X. Kercanaj. So, I decided to put it here since more people need to realize the obvious.

The Secret Covenant by UNKNOWN
An illusion it will be, so large, so vast it will escape their perception.

Those who will see it will be thought of as insane. We will create separate fronts to prevent them from seeing the connection between us. We will behave as if we are not connected to keep the illusion alive. Our goal will be accomplished one drop at a time so as to never bring suspicion upon ourselves. This will also prevent them from seeing the changes as they occur. We will always stand above the relative field of their experience for we know the secrets of the absolute. We will work together always and will remain bound by blood and secrecy. Death will come to him who speaks.

We will keep their lifespan short and their minds weak while pretending to do the opposite. We will use our knowledge of science and technology in subtle ways so they will never see what is happening. We will use soft metals, aging accelerators and sedatives in food and water, also in the air. They will be blanketed by poisons everywhere they turn. The soft metals will cause them to lose their minds. We will promise to find a cure from our many fronts, yet we will feed them more poison. The poisons will be absorbed through their skin and mouths, they will destroy their minds and reproductive systems. From all this, their children will be born dead, and we will conceal this information.

The poisons will be hidden in everything that surrounds them, in what they drink, eat, breathe and wear. We must be ingenious in dispensing the poisons for they can see far. We will teach them that the poisons are good, with fun images and musical tones. Those they look up to will help. We will enlist them to push our poisons. They will see our products being used in film and will grow accustomed to them and will never know their true effect. When they give birth we will inject poisons into the blood of their children and convince them it's for their help.

We will start early on, when their minds are young, we will target their children with what children love most sweet things. When their teeth decay we will fill them with metals that will kill their mind and steal their future. When their ability to learn has been affected, we will create medicine that will make them sicker and cause other diseases for which we will create yet more medicine. We will render them docile and weak before us by our power. They will grow depressed, slow and obese, and when they come to us for help, we will give them more poison.

We will focus their attention toward money and material goods so they may never connect with their inner self. We will distract them with fornication, external pleasures and games so they may never be one with the oneness of it all. Their minds will belong to us, and they will do as we say. If they refuse we shall find ways to implement mind-altering technology into their lives. We will use fear as our weapon. We will establish their governments and establish opposites within. We will own both sides. We will always hide our objective but carry out our plan. They will perform the labor for us, and we shall prosper from their toil. Our families will never mix with theirs. Our blood must be pure always, for it is the way.

We will make them kill each other when it suits us. We will keep them separated from the oneness by dogma and religion. We will control all aspects of their lives and tell them what to think and how. We will guide them kindly and gently letting them think they are guiding themselves. We will foment animosity between them through our factions. When a light shall shine among them, we shall extinguish it by ridicule, or death, whichever suits us best. We will make them rip each other's hearts apart and kill their own children. We will accomplish this by using hate as our ally, anger as our friend. The hate will blind them totally, and never shall they see that from their conflicts we emerge as their rulers.

They will be busy killing each other. They will bathe in their own blood and kill their neighbors for as long as we see fit. We will benefit greatly from this, for they will not see us, for they cannot see us. We will continue to prosper from their wars and their deaths. We shall repeat this over and over until our ultimate goal is accomplished. We will continue to make them live in fear and anger through images and sounds. We will use all the tools we have to accomplish this. The tools will be provided by their labor. We will make them hate themselves and their neighbors. We will always hide the divine truth from them, that we are all one. This they must never know!

They must never know that color is an illusion, they must always think they are not equal. Drop by drop, drop by drop we will advance our goal. We will take over their land, resources and wealth to exercise total control over them. We will deceive them into accepting laws that will steal the little freedom they will have. We will establish a money system that will imprison them forever, keeping them and their children in debt. When they shall ban together, we shall accuse them of crimes and present a different story to the world for we shall own all the media. We will use our media to control the flow of information and their sentiment in our favor.

When they shall rise up against us we will crush them like insects, for they are less than that. They will be helpless to do anything for they will have no weapons. We will recruit some of their own to carry out our plans, we will promise them eternal life, but eternal life they will never have for they are not of us. The recruits will be called "initiates" and will be indoctrinated to believe false rites of passage to higher realms.

Members of these groups will think they are one with us never knowing the truth. They must never learn this truth for they will turn against us. For their work they will be rewarded with earthly things and great titles, but never will they become immortal and join us, never will they receive the light and travel the stars. They will never reach the higher realms, for the killing of their own kind will prevent passage to the realm of enlightenment. This they will never know. The truth will be hidden in their face, so close they will not be able to focus on it until it's too late. Oh yes, so grand the illusion of freedom will be, that they will never know they are our slaves. When all is in place, the reality we will have created for them will own them. This reality will be their prison. They will live in self-delusion. When our goal is accomplished a new era of domination will begin.

Their minds will be bound by their beliefs; the beliefs we have established from time immemorial. But if they ever find out they are our equal, we shall perish then. THIS THEY MUST NEVER KNOW. If they ever find out that together they can vanquish us, they will take action.

They must never, ever find out what we have done, for if they do, we shall have no place to run, for it will be easy to see who we are once the veil has fallen. Our actions will have revealed who we are and they will hunt us down and no person shall give us shelter.

This is the secret covenant by which we shall live the rest of our present and future lives, for this reality will transcend many generations and life spans. This covenant is sealed by blood, our blood. We, the ones who from heaven to earth came.

```
This covenant must NEVER, EVER be known to exist.
It must NEVER, EVER be written or spoken of, for if
it is, the consciousness it will spawn will release
the fury of the PRIME CREATOR upon us and we shall
be cast to the depths from whence we came and remain
there until the end time of infinity itself.
```

In the above, they knew very well the power that WE THE PEOPLE possess. That's why they have done the impossible to poison people's mind, body and spirit for generations. We are in the end game, their game is over. We are in the transitioning stage. The transition from darkness to light.

> LIVE, LET GO. GO WITH THE FLOW THAT YOU
> CREATE, BUT ONLY WHEN YOU ARE A CONSCIOUS
> CREATOR.

PORN

8 Porn gives you an artificial overload of dopamine. It damage your brain cells. Watching porn on a regular basis halts your ability to be mentally aroused by the other gender since your energy will be focused on the sacral chakra, which means that your brain receptors/neurons are damaged, overloaded, over excited and you become numb and dumb.

Me and my husband were watching a lot of porn until 10 years ago. We were destroying ourselves, our mental, emotional and spiritual selves. Pornography is a form of mind control. Pornography is one of the most vile form of black magic. Porn is free because you are the product. You think you consume porn but it is porn that consumes you. You pay with your soul when watching degenerate dark magic content. Because you have pleasure watching/consuming something it does not mean that it is healthy. The black magicians running the planet know the power of semen and retaining it. They know that semen (conserving the sexual energy for both genders) is the key to awakening the Kundalini and all the spiritual powers that its awakening entails.

Samael Awn Weor writes in one of his books:

From the dawn of life, a great battle has raged between the powers of light and the powers of darkness. The secret root of the battle lies in sex. The correct interpretation of the mysteries of sex exists. The white magicians never ejaculate the semen. The black magician always ejaculate the semen. The white magicians make the igneous serpent of our magical powers ascend through the medullar canal. The black magicians make the snake descend towards the atomic infernos of the human being. Gods and demons live in eternal struggle. The Gods defend the doctrine of chastity. The demons hate chastity. In sex, the root of the conflict between Gods and demons is found.

The great battle takes place in the Astral Light. The Astral Light is the deposit of all great Nature's past, present, and future forms. The Astral Light is the Azoth and Magnesia of the ancient Alchemists, Medea's Flying Dragon, the Christians' INRI, the Tarot of the Bohemians. The

Astral Light is a terrific sexual fire springing forth from the Sun's nimbus and us fixed to the Earth by the force of gravity and the weight of the atmosphere.

The semen is the human beings Astral liquid. The semen is the Astral Light. The semen is the key to all powers and the key to all empires. The Astral Light has two poles, one positive and the other negative. The ascending serpent is positive. The descending serpent is negative. When it ascends, it is the brazen serpent that healed the Israelites in the wilderness. When it descends, it is the tempting serpent of Eden.

In the region of light, live the beings who adore each other. In the region of darkness live the souls who become inebriated with the chalice of lust, and who after getting drunk spill the cup. Those souls are consumed in the fire of their own lust.

I apologize, I do not remember which book of his this is from. I have a few of his books but I got this from a screenshot of one of his book pages I had in my cellphone. Nonetheless, I suggest you look into Samael Aun Weor's books.

Are you convinced yet that sexual energy is the most powerful thing in the universe? Sexual energy is meant to rise you up, enlighten you, unite you with the mirror counterparts of yourself. The dark magicians (those controlling humanity from behind the curtain) know very well the importance of conserving the sexual energy. Even though this part is talking about semen, about men, when a man is possessed, defeated, lost, has low self esteem, is emotionally imbalanced, not clear minded as a result of wasting their most precious substance/elixir a.k.a. semen, they will poison their wives, girlfriends, partners with whatever they have been poisoned with. Energy transference is real.

If you are a woman you should not allow a men within your sexual temple unless they are cleaned from all the trauma and poisons. The same thing applies to men, they (the cleaned ones) should not get together with un unhealed woman as she is carrying all the trauma, astral residues (poison/entities) from any man she has ever been with in the past. The more men she's been with, the heavier, denser, harmful the energy she carries. First step to cleaning yourself is to stay away from porn or any person, or social media accounts that post sexual pictures, comments and/or words.

You don't need to watch porn to be tempted sexually, it's enough that you see some skin in someone's posts or in real life if a woman is dressed provocatively. The same applies but less, if you are a woman since men are more "visually" than women. We are mental creatures, we need to be aroused mentally first, by the right mature intelligent self-aware men of course. If you spill your semen you fall, the only way to rise is to save your seed. For women, the equivalent wasting of the semen, is the blood and eggs. Do you think you are created to waste once a month the river of life (blood)? Let me put it in perspective, when you drink coffee you will have to urinate much faster/earlier as opposed to not having any coffee.

Urine, just as the blood, contains **stem cells, nutrients, minerals** which all these are important for the growth and the healing of the brain and other parts of your body. So, drinking coffee causes you to lose a wealth of internal **knowledge**. What causes the loss of blood once a month? Yes, you could say that the body has to clean itself for when the woman gets pregnant. And that is true to a certain extent. But that is simply a reaction/adjustment of the body that had to go through so that we survive as a species.

At one point in time, long time ago women didn't menstruate, their bodies were pure. Know that you may very well be carrying traits, elements, cells, memories etc. from up to 7 generations before this one. From one generation to the next, the human body has been degenerated even further, especially in the last decades. You will probably think that people live longer nowadays compared to the past. How do you know that in the past people didn't live longer? Because you were conditioned by the mainstream lies to think that we are living longer now, this way it stops you from questioning. People in the past lived for hundreds and thousands of years.

The two main things to live that long was "conserving sexual energy" and "fasting". Back in the day, before people were poisoned by lust, people were copulating with loving intention. But nowadays people have sexual intercourse for pleasure, which means that their energy gets stuck in the lower chakras, which means people are living in an animalistic nature.

ALCOHOL - A lot of people drink liquor/alcohol thinking that what they drink is good for them because it makes them feel good. Both alcohol and porn opens up your spiritual/astral body to be possessed by the most darkest and lowest of energy thought forms or entities. An alcoholic person that died would be attached to this kind of spirit (alcohol is a low frequency spirit), this Earthly dense plane is all they know so their spirit will roam around places that he used to frequent when he was alive, such as in bars, clubs, parties or any other places/houses where he had pleasure consuming (actually being consumed) by alcohol.

So, for example, if you purchased a used house where a deceased alcoholic lived, the spirit of that person would be in the house and most likely you will be possessed by him/her. When you read the word "possessed" what did you think? Did you think about the movie "Exorcist"? The kind of exorcism in that movie is exaggerated, even though it could happen like that but very rarely. The real exorcism is subtle, in the form of alcohol, porn, watching the fake news media, listening to other people without paying attention to your inner voice and many other subtle ways that this system has which numbs down people's brains. Oh, coffee is also another form of control.

There was an experiment done where some scientists gave different kinds of drugs (Caffeine, Marijuana, Benzedrine etc.) to spiders. The spider they gave coffee to, was the worst at building spiderwebs. This proves that coffee affected the spider's brain. Sugar and alcohol are the worst to be consumed because they consume you and not the other way around. While smoking and drinking coffee can mostly be bad for your physical health, sugar and alcohol can and will destroy your mental health. If medicine worked, you wouldn't need to refill your prescription. The majority of humanity that works for corporations begin their day with at least a cup of coffee. They begin their day with an acidic mind-numbing poison. I used to drink coffee every *morning (Rising).

Why do you think coffee is the number one drink people have in the morning/rising? Because it overloads the brain, it totally wakes you up (forcefully). Your system is designed to wake up incrementally and not abruptly. Since I stopped working for corporations, I barely drink any coffee. I eventually/soon will completely stop drinking coffee. It is one thing to have coffee consciously, once in a while and another thing to have coffee daily because of being addicted to it.

In the book *SELF EMPOWERMENT – BOOK 1* by Saimir Kercanaj, I read an interesting chapter about the importance of not saying "Good Morning" instead we should say "**Grand Rising** or **Supreme Rising**" or " **New Rising**" or "**New day** or **Good day**".

EVERY SINGLE ONE OF US CASTS SPELLS ANYTIME WE SPEAK. The

whole English language is a spell. During our everyday life, the phrases we are programmed to say regularly are hexes. Just by saying the simple phrase "good morning", you are being hexed. Most are oblivious to this hidden in plain sight devious control scheme. "Grand rising" is the best way to greet people. The word morning derives from mourning. The word morning is a homophone for "mourning" which means "grieving". You would not want to start the day with mourning, would you? Of course not.

This phrase casts a spell to make people feel defeated, lost, and hopeless and to feel like they suffered a loss even if they didn't suffer a loss. These (and many others) spell casting words weaken your psyche. Another spell casting word is "week." You go to work at your job (job means persecution in Hebrew) all week (which phonetically sounds as WEAK), to earn (URN=holds the ashes of the dead) your check and you can't wait for the weekend (WEAKENED).

Many can't wait for the weekend as they are already exhausted giving their life energy to the parasites (those controlling behind the scenes). They are leeches living off your blood.

They (the ones that wanted total control of humanity) kept the knowledge to themselves. Technically you can't blame them because they did not force you to work. You got caught in the middle of a huge web of lies and deceit. The moment you start blaming is the moment you lost the race, the game called life. Don't you think that it is time to pay attention to how you express yourself? Instead of saying "good morning", say "good day" or "grand rising".

Do you see how nice they sound? They sound empowering. When you say, "Can't wait for weekend", besides the word weekend that sounds as "weakened", you also condition yourself to be demoralized even from the second part of the word which is "end". Nothing ends. And nothing begins. To know that something begins, it implies that there is also an ending. I innerstand that a week begins on a Monday and ends on Sunday, although the week should start on a Sunday as the Sun is the beginning of everything in the day. I innerstand that you need to drive somewhere that is let's say 30km away, of course there is a beginning and an ending to the trip. That's not the point of this explanation about the spell casting subject. The point is to substitute disempowering words and phrases with positive, empowering ones.

SIZE DOESN'T MATTER

There are two kinds of women, those that live in the body and those that get aroused by intelligence and emotional maturity. Porn makes many men feel defeated about their size. As a woman I can tell you that size does not matter, how you use it does. But even then, your mind is what matters, how you talk, whether you have an open heart, a clear mind or not. When there is real love between a couple, there are no flaws. Do you want to know why people find flaws with each other? First, it's because you compare your partner with your ex-partners. One partner had a better smile, or was taller, or skinnier or more understanding etc. Or you (your subconscious) compare with sizes in porn movies you have watched.

Everyone is beautiful, but first you must realize that you are beautiful and perfect before finding perfection in others. Unless there is genuine love between a couple, one or the other will find flaws with each other. Unless you are honest to yourself, you will keep lying to yourself and others. As for "size doesn't matter" men too have their preferences about women's breast size or their behind. Where do these preferences/comparisons come from? They come from being stuck in the carnal and animalistic world. Porn or any other sexualization content contributes in the destruction of family values.

Alberto (the husband) is taking over now for a bit.
In the past I met a woman (we stayed together for 6 months) with tiny breasts and her behind was not as good as I would have liked. She was the most lovable woman I had ever met up until that time. She made me laugh, she understood me, she was fun to hang around with. But because I was poisoned by pornography I strayed away and was looking for women with more beautiful bodies, which I ended up with someone else which I had pleasure only in sex. I have friends that are together or married to gorgeous women, and yet these friends (which I rarely meet up anymore) are cheating on them.

They watch porn constantly and are artificially aroused and since they have been for a while with these women, they are bored and are looking for other women. There is no love in their relationships, at least not reciprocal one. The point is that one should look at the overall picture when choosing a partner and not just the physical part. You can enjoy and have pleasure with a very sexy person, but what about when you don't have sex? What are you going to talk about? If there is no communication, then the ship is sinking.

"IF YOU WANT TO DESTROY ANY NATION WITHOUT WAR, MAKE ADULTERY OR NUDITY COMMON IN THE YOUNG GENERATION." - KENNETH SALADIN

IF YOU MASTURBATE TO PORNOGRAPHIC CONTENT YOU ARE NOT A COMPLETE MAN

9 There is an agenda to keep men and women slaves to their carnal pleasures by promoting anything sexual including that masturbating is healthy or that retaining semen causes prostate cancer. These are false. Just ask yourself, why do you masturbate? What's the reason? What is it that you are lacking? Is the intention yours or a result of outside forces or conditioning? Always remember that what is normal doesn't mean that it is healthy or true. The same can be applied for the opposite too, but much less, since in this world low frequency products or activities have become the norm. Your energy must fully flow throughout all your energy centers (chakras) and not be focused only (mostly) on the 2nd one which is the Sacral Chakra.

Having the urge to masturbate derives from you lacking real love/sex, or you are too invested in sexuality and that's all you know on how to cope with lack of love. If your keep lying to yourself, you are shattering the truth even further. **The sooner you take responsibility for your actions, the sooner you'll collect the broken shards** (pieces of truths lost along the way).

> Porn desensitizes you from life, you get a constant overload of dopamine which makes it hard for you to enjoy the normal things, just as watching movies and news channels desensitize you from being empathetic

since you are bombarded so much with wars, death and
immorality that it becomes normal in your brain,
so when someone dies in wars or otherwise, it is
nothing for you, you don't get enraged for the
unjust deaths that occur. The death of someone that
you don't know, it is not any less important than
the death of someone that you know/love. Think about
it...

I write what I write from a deeper life meaning point of view, from a spiritual perspective. You cannot deny the fact that you will eventually destroy yourself if you keep your sexual energy concentrated (including dissipating it) instead of allowing it to flow throughout all your system as intended. A real man is a complete package and not operating from an animalistic lower mind.

Test yourself and see if you are on the right path, test whether you can control your lust and hunger. Lust and hunger are the most difficult and important for a man to become a MAN. If this chapter's title triggered you in a bad way, then it is clear that you must see it as an opportunity to do something about it. Every time you ejaculate your soul is enslaved further, your kundalini which is coiled at the base of your spine falls deeper asleep. The deeper asleep it goes the more difficult it will be to awaken it, let alone raising it up to your pineal gland. This applies the same for women.

The Kundalini will not rise if your sexual energy is wasted externally. There is white and dark magic. You and everyone is a magician. Most people are lousy magicians where they create their reality out of ignorance. When you know that you possess the ELIXIR OF LIFE (in this case "*semen/sexual energy-the most potent universal raw energy*"), you wouldn't want to waste it, but instead you would use it to create consciously.

> "**Excessive loss/waste of semen as a result of
> frequent intercourse/masturbation with ejaculation,
> is the prime cause of impotence in men.**" From the
> book *Body Mind Soul-As You Believe So Shall It Be* page198 by
> Saimir Kercanaj

If you are a teenager and you want to explore your sexual body parts, that is okay and understandable (as long as you don't ejaculate). But when you are a grown up man and masturbate to people on the screen having sex, it totally captures your consciousness. The more you watch porn (or even having sex with just anyone or a lot) the harder it will be to get the sexual energy to travel back up the spine. Orgasm is the little death. Just as you age slowly where you don't notice the aging since you see youself daily in the mirror, so does ejaculating (including just orgasms) ages you slowly without you realizing that you are the cause that you age and die as a result of your habits/poisons and undisciplined daily life.

Conserving the sexual energy is one of the most kept secret since the ancient times. If the title of this chapter triggers you, that is a good indication that you must do something about it, meaning to become a self-conscious person where your choices derive from a clear mind as opposed to from confusion and ignorance of self. Unleash the full potential that you possess.

As a man you must build every day, you must create every day, you must be your natural authentic self. If you don't, you will succumb to instant gratification in the form of meaningless sex & masturbation, liquor, fantasy screen time (videogames, TV shows, movies etc), and many others foolish activities that will rob the soul out of you. Build a hobby. Build a career, only if it has to do with helping freeing humanity, otherwise any other career offered by the mainstream establishment is only to divide and conquer us. Build your body, build your mind. Not many men build their knowledge, even fewer build a passion. Many men go weeks, months and years without building anything because they are defeated mentally/spiritually. They waste their life away. Don't be that man, be better. Do better. Unleash/honor your masculinity so that women feel safe and protected where children and any generation after will have a bright future

TEST YOURSELF: ACHIEVE A 6 MONTH-PERIOD WITHOUT EJACULATING. WITHOUT SEX. AND WITHOUT ORGASM. ARE YOU STRONG ENOUGH TO DO IT? YOU MAY LIFT BIG WEIGHTS BUT THE REAL STRENGTH IS MENTAL.

MALE/FEMALE ATTRACTION

10 Naturally we are created to be attracted to each other heterosexually. Everything in the known universe functions in both feminine and masculine energies. Even the appliances in your house function through this male/female fact. Even though a man and a woman couple are heterosexual, they could still have big problems in their relationship. Out of many reasons, one of them is that either the man is a beta male or the woman has been masculinized. You cannot beat the universal system. Balance of both sexual energies must be achieved.

Many men think that because they love sex/women, that makes them real men. To want to have sex is the most basic function of a man. To be a real man you must think for yourself, you must be emotionally balanced, you must have a clear mind, to not have low self esteem and to be a protector of women. Don't just be attracted to women when you want to have sex. Sex should be your last concern. Arouse a woman's mind and she is all yours.

Ovulating women produce a scent known as "copulance/copulence." A team of scientists found that when men were exposed to small amounts of copulance, they were unable to distinguish attractive female faces from unattractive ones.

What does this suggest? It suggests [according to my 100% assumption] that this substance repels the opposite gender since naturally two people should mate with genuine intention, from the heart and not based on external appearances. In modern times both men and women load themselves (women usually much more than men) with make up, perfumes, deodorants, lipstick and a lot of other lab made hormone disruptor poisons which then confuses the opposite gender. Men and women release pheromones.

Rimias K. Neo in his book *GAIN WISDOM THROUGH PRACTICED KNOWLEDGE* says this about the pheromones:

*W*hat are pheromones? Pheromones are chemicals that humans and animals use to communicate. Your body releases pheromones through urine, sweat, semen, breast milk and vaginal fluids. These pheromone chemicals are responsible for you to attract the opposite gender/mate. If you attract the same gender but you know for sure that you are 100% heterosexual then you are fine, it is them that are poisoned. But even then, if you hang around regularly with homosexuals, then they will poison you, not on purpose of course.

Just think about it, use your imagination. They are no better than you, and you are no better then them. We all are divine, it's just that their motherboard has been hijacked. If you are attracted to the same gender, then you've been hijacked, been injected with a virus, in the form of movies, tv shows, magazines, tap water, perfumes, chemically produced foods etc. You can undo anything, you can reverse anything, including homosexuality. Check the subchapter about homosexuality. Using a perfume on you will confuse your natural senses and you will not be able to sense the male pheromones. If you are a man and you put deodorant on you, it applies the same, your pheromones will not be sensed by a strong divine and intelligent woman.

Humans have a rational mind, and the mind can be hijacked. Many women or men get together with a partner based on how they look, what they possess, what job they do etc. Animals don't do that. Wearing perfume, deodorant, make up, hair gel etc., not only you cannot sense/attract a strong mate, but you may attract the same gender [homosexuality]. You may already be a heterosexual man/woman, but by wearing these things on a regular basis, you affect people at work, at shopping places, family members, especially yours or someone else's children. These chemicals exist not just to block odor, but to influence someone's mind. These chemicals affect one's critical thinking, emotions and even sexual preference.

Those that want humans to remain slaves, know very well how to poison children's minds. First they poison the parents and then the children are automatically poisoned. Animals act on natural instinct. Animals mate only with the strongest. So, begin to shed off the poisons that you've been putting on yourself for a long time. It is time to question anything that society deems to be normal. Normal is slavery, poison and death.

Do you have what it takes to undo the damage that you have done and are still doing to yourself and others?

My husband rarely wears any deodorant, but when he does, I'm repelled, I cannot sense his pheromones. Pheromones signal to a woman his masculinity. A true Alpha male doesn't put on him any deodorant, gel or anything that has chemicals in it, or any at all. The same applies to women that wear make up, perfume etc., they will push Alpha males away, they will only attract wounded men, children in grown up bodies, men that miss their mother.

There are at least 2 reasons that men and women put/wear makes up, deodorant, perfume etc., to attract the opposite gender and for the purpose of hygiene. Whichever the reason is, you push away the other person. If you use perfume/deodorant to cover the smell, then you should have a shower more often. Speaking of having a shower, use unscented soap/shampoo/conditioner, otherwise the smell of those products will confuse the other gender. You may say that even if you shower you may still smell bad in hot weather. The reason that your sweat smells is because of what you eat. I speak from experience. Stop consuming store-bought processed foods and drinks, with the exception of fruit, vegetables, herbs, nuts and filtered water.

So pretty much stop eating anything that doesn't grow from the ground. And even then, you better fast regularly and you'll see that eventually you will not smell anymore. Out of many reasons why couples end up breaking up and/or cheating on each other, one of the reasons is fake, poison products that people put on themselves. As a woman, I barely put any make up on, only when I go to work. Writing is my part time hobby; I still work for a corporation until I'm ready to work for myself. Going back to wearing make up, when I get home, I wash it off, I do not want my husband to smell fakeness. I don't need to hide anything from him and I shouldn't have to hide anything from anyone else either. So, soon I will stop wearing any make up at all.

If you are a woman reading this chapter, I can tell you with certainty that you can never keep a man from cheating on you if you are not 100% honest to yourself about your weight, your emotions, your thoughts, intentions and overall outlook. In case you didn't know, a woman is created to only mate with one man and vice versa. Having a child is an amazing thing, but when a child is a result of a mistake, it will affect the child's life and his/her grandchildren.

Just as our struggle in life is a result of our parent/grandparents ignorance. Please, do not be triggered, do not think with your emotions. Loving your parents or siblings doesn't mean that you should not know or realize their ignorance/flaws.

> We all are flawed one way or another, not by divine design but by man made design. The flaws that we have are little viruses that have been injected in us in the form of **government, organized religion, legal documentation, feminism agend**a, **skin color racism,** *equality, **voting, lab made so called foods and drinks, fluoridated water** and many more forms of poisons that have captured people's minds and spirits.

*EQUALITY – This is a major poison. This is part of an agenda to disrupt and destroy relationships. In the past I was infected by this agenda to the point that I was raising my voice at my ex-partner, and a couple of times I was about to raise my hand to him. He was a genuinely strong man. He was way beyond my level. He saw potential in me and was very patient with me, but eventually he disappeared and left. If I had raised a hand on him, what do you think, would I be able to win? Of course not, my mind was poisoned at that time. I had strayed away from the feminine gender role.

Eventually I began hanging around with people that were working on improving themselves, this way I got back on track, in honoring my feminine role. This was just a simple example that was not a major harm since at that time I didn't have any children. I personally know a couple of women (ex friends) that attacked their partners with legality, they took their children, house and everything away. These women inflicted bad karma (check again the 1st page of the chapter "KARMA =ACTION") on themselves. It is one thing to take someone's materialistic things, and another to take away the child. A child came through you but not from you. It is not our call to take the child away from the mother or from the father, with the exception when the parent is an alcoholic or in anyway that could put child's life in danger. I only mentioned two examples on how relationships can be destroyed.

There are countless of situations where destruction can easily happen. A woman must honor her role, just as men have to. But for two people to be the right one for each other, they must begin the first step by being honest and genuine to themselves and to the other gender/partner. When my not-yet husband asked me out I went on a date without wearing any make up or perfume. I did not want to begin a relationship with lies. It is true that the heart and the mind are very important, but what you wear and what you say is a result of your thoughts which then manifests into actions. I gladly cook and take care of him, that's my job as intended by the intelligent design/creation. He cooks too but when it's about fixing or building things in the house or around the house, he doesn't cook, he honors his masculine role. He takes his son with him and teaches him to be a man, just as I keep my daughter with me, teaching her to become a woman.

Men are good at some things; women are good at other things. Both divine qualities of men and women put together, makes the union powerful. Those in power do not want a strong union between women and men that's why they have feminized men and masculinized women through many different nefarious tactics. Where I used to work, I saw two married men one time that ate instant noodles for lunch. That is poison food. I cry inside when I see them eat that, many times I bring them home made food. Isn't that sad? These married men were betrayed by their wives' feminine. I am not saying that their wives did it on purpose. These wives are children from parents that were already at the point of no return, meaning people with severely poisoned mind.

Take care of your partner/husband, and he should also take care of you by being the provider and the protector. If you earn more then him, it is fine. Better less money and have more time available with the family. Many men work 12 hours a day, earn a lot of money (a big chunk of that is taxes), they have to drive for 2 hours to work and back home. When they get home they are exhausted and may not have time for you and the children. This is a subject that I could go on and on about. I hope you get the point that each gender (male and female) must fully honour their roles. There is no other way to freedom.

In the past when I was not true to myself, I controlled my partner and I paid for it. But now I feel good about honoring my gender's role and taking care of my husband. I also help other men (with advice) anyway I can because I see many couples can fix the relationship but they do not know where to start. I feel it is my duty as a human and as a female to help humanity as much as possible. This is one of the reasons that caused me to write a book in hopes that some people may be empowered on improving their daily life. Men are the masters of the physical world; women are the masters of the spiritual world. When you realize this, you will be on the right track to balancing yourself, meaning masculine and feminine balance.

"When you have sex, you use all 5 senses, therefore you are contained within the 5 sense reality. It's one thing to make reciprocated love and another to have sex just to satisfy the bodily pleasures. Love is made from the soul. Sex is simply to satisfy the senses or procreate, which is the animalistic lower form of procreation, with the highest form of procreation being PARTHENOGENESIS (virgin birth)"

Arolv Jae, *THE TREASURE WITHIN*, p136

LET YOUR BODY EMIT IT'S ORIGINAL DIVINE SCENT. OTHERWISE YOU'LL CONFUSE THE OPPOSITE GENDER BUT ALSO THE SAME GENDER.

ORGASM DERIVED FROM LUST (FOLLOWED BY EJACULATION) IS THE DEATH OF MASCULINITY

WRITTEN BY MY HUSBAND

11 When you achieve [naturally or as a result of the urges] paroxysmal or intense excitement or otherwise known as orgasm, your consciousness is killed for a short moment, which consequently takes a chunk out of your lifespan. This rapid pleasurable release of neuromuscular tension at the height of sexual excitement is accompanied by ejaculation of semen for men and by vaginal contractions in women. These few moments of sexual climax results in binding you in the dense realm. No matter how pleasurable it may be, you can still be killed (mentally and spiritually slowed down) by low negative energy field entities. To many people, alcohol is pleasurable and yet their life is forfeited. To many others sports are a form of pleasure and yet they use their time to be distracted instead on working on self-mastery. Death can come in many forms.

When the expulsion of semen happens, an induction happens, in the form of male reproductive cycle.

This reproductive cycle can also be seen as a male period. You may see the word *"period"* as nonsense because you associate that word only with women but try to understand the bigger picture. In men, every time an orgasm (followed by ejaculation) happens there are psychological consequences. Just as women have psychological/emotional consequences during their menstrual cycle or period. These emotional consequences manifest as depression, irritability, fatigue, mood fluctuations, less concentration, heightened impatience and also removing themselves from society, it makes them vulnerable. So as you can see, these symptoms happen to both genders.

When you lose or waste your seminal fluids your capacity is severely reduced. When you lack full capacity as a man, you have much less potential to provide and protect your family. Well, many men work all day long, every day to provide for their wife and children, but many of them are weak in front of her, getting abused by her, mentally, emotionally, but also these men do not have the time to spend with their children or friends. In many relationships, the wife doesn't allow their husband/boyfriend to hang around with their male friends. What does this tell you? Do not blame the woman. She is what you attracted.

Any strong and intelligent woman would respect a real Alpha man that is clear minded, emotionally mature with a head above his shoulders. Many of these incapacitated men, then resort to alcohol and of course porn, where their mind is possessed and steered toward immoral fantasies that eventually would cause these men to expect the same from their wives. It is one thing to want to try new things with a partner that you love genuinely, and another when something external, in this case porn introduces poison in the relationship. All this could be avoided if semen is not wasted. Semen loss equals loss of intelligence.

When women have their period, they are not themselves, the same applies to men. It seems more apparent in women because they lose their focus those few days in the menstrual cycle, but men lose it in chunks, over a course of a few or many ejaculations in one month.

One single ejaculation in one month, equals one period for women. If men ejaculate more than once a month, then men are automatically weaker than women. So, technically men have periods too, not real periods but you know what I mean, as in men wasting their life elixir, just as women waste their blood and eggs.

If you are a man, you know that after ejaculation you (usually most men) will temporary lose interest in her, either you will sleep, or lie beside her without the same energy/magnetism that you had prior to losing your life force or semen. And then, eventually you will be interested in her when your nuts become full again. This is animalistic life/carnal pleasure. There is a reason why you have a brain, to use it and not to lose it.

Every time you ejaculate, you not only lose intelligence, but also a piece of your soul. When you have an orgasm, a piece of your soul escapes through the portal that opens in the moment of the climax. Orgasm is called *"the little death"* **in French.**

It applies to both genders. This whole thing applies to both women and men, but I named this chapter this way to emphasize that men too, have their own period time. The exception here is "tantric sex". In tantric sex where love is made with genuine intention without losing the creative sexual energy externally. All energy remains and circulate internally where connection with the Source of all is established, meaning that you have access to the void or the source of everything, you become one with it.

If you are a men that has ejaculated regularly for many years and has a family, children a job etc., you may think that your life is fine. Is it? What do you feel when cops drive by you while you are driving, or when they pull you over? What did you feel when you had to wear a mask/muzzle when Covid [renamed Flu] was going on? What do you feel when your job/position could be in danger of losing it as a result of many factors?

What do you feel when you think, imagine, assume that your girlfriend or wife may have gone or might go with another man? The answer to the above questions (which you will have to answer) will tell you if you have [or had] a period. I call it a period because of the feminization of men that has been going for a long time, especially in the recent decades.

You can forge your destiny by the steps you take and not by the shoes you wear. You can wear golden shoes but if you don't know which direction you have to go, you'll still be lost, no matter how many steps you take.

Every time you have an orgasm, you completely lose your consciousness for a couple or more seconds. In those seconds you are connected to the astral realm. When you have an orgasm from having watched porn or if you had sex with an unhealed women (or a man if you are a woman), low vibrational fields or entities can and will drip/enter your field and become a part of you. The more you open that portal (orgasmal moment), the stronger the pull that you will have on those dark/low frequency entities. You may feel good for a bit when you have an orgasm but you are paying with your life. You can totally ignore what I'm saying and go back to destroying yourself even further. But you are the one losing, no matter how much you ignore the problem, you cannot escape from it unless you face it. Just as there are good and not so good people in the physical world, so are there good and not so good entities in the astral worlds (the non-physical realities).

You may ask: *"If orgasm is bad, why did the creator create it to feel so good?"* The creator (or whatever it is that created everything) created the orgasm only for the purpose of procreation, so that you feel good when having a child. This applies when both men and women have an orgasm at the same time when they are trying to have a child. Most couples don't have an orgasm at the exact same time because of many factors, one of them is stress, then there are other factors such as, bad foods, drinks, drugs, porn, hormone pills, lack of knowledge etc. All these contribute to men and women not being in sync with each other. Sex was originally meant for procreation and not for pleasure. Sex has been abused for a long time and look at society now, it has been declining for a long time, since the beginning of the sexual energy abuse.

In the book **Rebuild Yourself From Within** by J.J. and TAMO, the authors state:

> "Masturbation, also commonly known as self-abuse, is the greatest of all sexual evils, not only because of its widespread practice and the opportunity for excesses, but especially because of the fact that it generally works its harm during the period of growth, when the results of any sexual mistake or abuse are far more serious than they would be in adult life."

The practice is detrimental at any phase of life, however, due to the drain upon the organism and the weakening or fatigue of the nerve centers which it implies. With semen retention, we recover our vitality and constitution one day at a time. Masturbation is genuinely an assault against the body to such a degree that the ramifications are not just bodily, but moral or emotional as well.

The mind and soul of the victim appear to be polluted at the same time as the body is weakened and sexual strength reduced by this horrible practice. Masturbation is frequently regarded to be more detrimental to males than to girls, because of the direct drain upon the resources of the body in the case of the male via the loss of the seminal fluid.

The resources drainage of women equivalent to men is their menstruation time when it occurs once a month. If men ejaculated no more than once a month, then they would be as strong as women. I'm not speaking about muscle strength here. But because men lose their life force in chunks over a period of time (a few ejaculations a month) they feel like they are not drained, but instead they are destroyed. Let me put it this way, **if you are a man and ejaculate at least 12/13 times in one month, it is equivalent to the energy/life force that a woman loses in a whole year**. If women had a period every time they orgasmed (*assuming if they masturbated/had sex the same times as men*), then that would be the end of life as we know it. It is already bad as it is. But it can be easily fixed if you really put the effort. YOU CAN DO IT...

> ORGASM/SEX OR PORN IS NO DIFFERENT THAN ALCOHOL IS TO AN ALCOHOLIC, OR ANY OTHER ADDICTION.

SEMEN RETENTION

12 Most of this subject is written by my husband Alberto. He is not a writer, I just asked him to help with this subject from his perspective as a man. If you are already practicing semen retention or if you haven't had sex for a long time as a result of not having found a girlfriend/woman, be extra careful to whom you engage sexually with. Because your body will be so hungry that you could fall in love immediately with the wrong person without having a clue who she is. Men's and woman's genitals are directly connected with the heart, that's why many times people fall in love when they have sex. And that is fine if she/he is the right person so don't engage sexually with just anyone.

You could fall in love even if you just kiss each other or even if you just met someone online after a few conversations. If she is someone that uses her sexual power to tempt, seduce, conquer you, avoid her like the plague. A real genuine Goddess would use her femininity to heal you, to empower you and not to make you lose your mind. A real feminine must help you keep your head above your shoulders and not make you lose it. After a long time of no sexual interaction with the opposite sex partner, anyone would seem like the greatest sexual encounter ever. It's like having fast food after being stuck without food for a whole month. The fast food would seem like the greatest thing you've ever eaten.

Depending on if you haven't had sex in a long time whether you were not capable or not lucky, but also depends on if you chose to not have sex for a long time by choice, assuming you would be on semen retention journey. In the later case you wouldn't make a mistake because you would be a clear minded person and you would not fall for just anyone just because you haven't had sex for a long time.

In the winter you must not ejaculate at all. But hey, up to you, you are the cure or the poison. If you haven't gained the mental strength yet to retain, at least try this technique I found in the book **BODY MIND SOUL** by Saimir Kercanaj. This is from the chapter ORGASMING WITHOUT EJACULATING – SEMEN RETENTION from the book I just mentioned.

This is something that all men should practice. Whether by themselves or with their partner. With the pointing and middle finger of the left hand (assuming you are right-handed) press hard between your anus and scrotum and keep your fingers there. To know what part I am talking about, just when you pee, put your two fingers at that spot and start urinating, stop the pee, let the pee go and stop it again, and you will see that muscle contracting.

It's where you should press hard as that place is the canal where semen passes through toward the exit into giving you a surface external temporary pleasure. Starting 15-20sec before having an orgasm and keep your fingers pressed hard there until 15-20 sec after the orgasm is finished. When the orgasm is finished (with the fingers still pressing), close your eyes, breathe deeply, fully, and visualize the semen going up the spine every time you inhale after the so-called amazing feeling of the orgasm is finished. Keep inhaling and exhaling slowly for the duration of 15-20sec. You will not lose a single drop, guaranteed.

Be aware that this technique is just a first step. Not wasting the seed is good, but getting aroused will concentrate your creative energy on the sacral chakra which conflicts with raising the kundalini. The end goal must be to not ejaculate at all until you pass away but also no orgasms ever again, unless you perform white tantric sex of course. In that case the orgasm is internal for both partners, where no energy gets lost/wasted externally.

```
Moses remained on mount Sinai for 40 days and 40
nights where he talked to God. There are many
interpretations of this but one of them is a
metaphor for resisting carnal/bodily pleasures/
temptations for 40 days and 40 nights. After these
many days, you become a new person, you meet the
Creator, you go within when you do this properly. No
sex, no masturbation, no arousal, no alcohol or any
man made foods or drinks.
```

To not have sex, or food for 40 days it seems impossible. Fasting for

3 days seemed impossible for me because I hadn't fasted before. But now, I can easily fast for one or two weeks. The point is that you must incrementally improve on anything that you want to achieve. If you want to master your spiritual life you must conquer the base desires, when you do that, you transform them into conscious virtues. I will not write much about fasting in this book but if you wish, I suggest you read the book *"THE TREASURE WITHIN"* by Leon H. Art where he writes a lot about fasting, meditation etc. The book *BODY MIND SOUL* that I previously mentioned, also talks about fasting, check that one out too.

Retaining your semen is not an easy task. The solution to any problem begins where the problem originated from, which is in the mind. Life is not just sex. Beauty is everywhere. You can walk, run, exercise in general, admire the flowers/plants. Walk in the park, climb a mountain, play a musical instrument even if you think you cannot learn how to play, which you can if you put effort on it. Life is full of beautiful things that you can enjoy. If you resort to porn or sex in general for pleasure then you have not understood the meaning of life.

Anything you cannot do without, is an addiction. Do you think that the life problems of an alcoholic will vanish simply by drinking alcohol. You will only postpone the inevitabile which is having to face the problem. Most problems are not existent, they are made up, in the mind. In the case of sex or masturbation, the problem is that your sexual energy is concentrated at the base of your spine, including the sacral chakra center. The energy must flow all along the spine feeding all chakras or the energy centers. Being addicted to anything is a blockage or a suppression of energy. When something is blocked, you eliminate what is causing the blockages.

If you watch porn or any sexualization online content, then something caused you to go there. It could be your thoughts, memories, or images of naked or semi naked people you see in other people's posts in social media accounts, or Tv, posters, movies etc. To starve the beast you must stop feeding it. Delete anyone that posts anything that tempts you to think sexually. An image or even a single word is like a sliver that will keep you bleeding until you take the sliver out.

RELAPSE REMEDY
When you practice semen retention, a lot of sexual energy is accumulated in the body. Sexual energy is creative energy and it

needs to be used by creating, otherwise you will relapse. If you have sex or masturbate, that's wasting the creative energy as opposed to using the accumulated energy (when you don't waste it through sex/masturbation). So you better learn how to draw, or play a musical instrument or learn how to cook or anything creative. Do anything new that is out of the ordinary so that your mind becomes excited by newness. So, pretty much exercise your mind/consciousness by doing new activities (physical or mental), keep your mind busy with creativity where all your senses are used, including your 6th sense the "*pineal gland*".

You may watch creative activities online but that is only half of the solution, you must also act on what you learn. It doesn't mean that you have to do everything you watch on the internet. Just pick one thing that you like to use as a creative activity and go for it. Just by watching a screen, you are only using your eyes and ears. But when you actually do something creative, you also use your hands which are energy extensions of your mind.

Your hands complete the work, or your hands water the seed. The seed is the information that you learned from others which consequently turn it into wisdom by practicing what you learned. Unless you keep yourself busy with creativity, you will always relapse.

    Even if you are strong to not relapse
    consciously, you will relapse in your sleep, in
    the form of wet dreams.

Your sexual energy is very potent, if it gets accumulated in the same spot (as in the lower part of your body), eventually it will explode, causing you to want to have sex or masturbate or you'll have wet dreams. The semen when not ejaculated, is absorbed by the cerebro spinal fluid that flows along your spine. You will age and die earlier if you waste your semen.

Beat sexual urges by:
Cold showers
Exercise
Turn off Wi-Fi/home internet but also turn it off while engaging in sexual activity.
No alcohol or any other acidic food or drinks.
Only engage in sexual activity with the opposite gender.
No masturbation.

No porn.
Deep conscious breathing.

*This is related to the kundalini which requires two opposites to be fully activated and raised. Male to male and/or female to female is undivine. Wrong or right is relative to each individual. My concern is divinity. Only through divine connection to the opposite genders can there ever be a utopian society. Male to male or female to female sex will never complete the battery effect that completes the circle of energy. It's how it is designed from divine intervention and it's how it will always be. I don't make the universal rules.

Semen retention is deeply rooted in ancient wisdom. It serves to preserve physical vitality and serves as a catalyst in your spiritual and intellectual growth. Many famous athletes, namely Mohammed Ali abstained from sex. Dodging the ladies gives you stamina, you build faster reaction time, you build energy, testosterone. The longer you abstain the stronger you become.

And this is not just related to athletes as in becoming only physically strong, but also mentally and emotionally. Semen retention is a strict "sexual discipline". Celibacy and tantric sex have been practiced since the beginning of time by humans, by those that had the knowledge. But having the knowledge of semen retention importance is not enough. A lot of people know things but are too lazy to work on themselves, on becoming stronger mentally, physically and spiritually. Porn exists only for one purpose, to diminish your soul's light. You are the LIGHT. **Your physical body is simply Light in physical form**.

Men who watch porn and play videogames for many hours a day will look down on drug addicts as if they are beneath them. They have the same problem as drug addicts. It's just the delivery source is different. Anything you consume for many hours a day is a drug, regardless of what society deemed it to be, legal or illegal. Coffee, medications, sugar, table salt are legal and yet, these are drugs.

PRACTICING DEEP BREATHING. SOLITUDE. FASTING. COLD
SHOWERS AND BEING AWAY FROM DIGITAL DEVICES (SOCIAL
MEDIA. INTERNET) WILL WORK WONDERS IN BEING ABLE TO
RETAIN FOR EVER.

CHASTITY OR POLYGAMY?

13 Whether you are a man or a woman, before opening your fortress (sexually) to the person you are interested in, ask them these questions:

1. *Do you think for yourself?*
2. *Do you love animals?*
3. *Do you consume meat?*
4. *Do you have empathy toward all sentient beings?*
5. *Are you a materialistic person?*
6. *Are you controlled by sexual urges?*
7. *Are you taking care of your body, mind and spirit?*
8. *Do you consume liquor? (any amount of alcohol is bad).*
9. *Do you fast?*
10. *Do you practice sexual alchemy (semen retention)?*

There are many more questions that you could ask but these are some on the top of my head. These things alone, if followed can radically change one's life for the better.

Questions #2 and #3 cannot be both answered with a "YES", they would be conflicting each other. You cannot be a virgin and a prostitute at the same time.

By the way, the word "prostitute" used here is not to be condescending. Prostitution exists because ignorance exists. When men learn how to control their urges and when women learn that money and materialism is poverty, then prostitution will disappear. Sure, some women do it for survival but there is no reason in our abundant world to need to survive. Ignorance of SELF and greed (generally speaking of our society) has caused these women to sell their most pressious possession for money. We all are guilty or have been guilty at one point or another in time, by having been consumerists which has contributed in the greed of mega corporations and businesses in general. Which in turn has caused poverty (physical and/or mental) among the masses. Minimize supporting greed and watch how everyone's life will improve.

Monogamy="LIFE" if you have understood the meaning of life, your purpose which means that you are healed from all addictions (*anything you cannot do without is an addiction*) including "lust".

Polygamy="DEATH" if you have not understood the meaning of life. It is all about what you wish in life, joy or pleasure. Monogamy with the right person is JOY that lasts. Multiple partners (not necessarily at the same time) means pleasure that is short lived. Joy and pleasure are not the same thing. Pleasure is about the senses, the physical part of you. Joy is from the heart, from the depths of your soul.

Let's say that you live a polygamous life for 20-30 years. In the context of how long people live nowadays, 20-30 years seems like a lot. When you think about your eternal soul's life span, these 20-30 years is but a single grain of sand in the grand scheme of things. In the end, it is up to you how you drink the poison, diluted or undiluted. Most men think that humans are polygamous because that has become the norm, they think it is natural for men to go with more than one woman. Look at our society, cheating left and right, children are not getting raised properly.

A lot of drama and struggling between most couples. Why? Because people's minds have been tainted by lust and seeking temporary pleasure. Any partner you go with, energy transference happens. The less unhealed partner will drain the energy of the other one and will transfer astral/energetic residues into each other. The same applies if both partners are on the righteous path and when they have sex (actually love) they will heal each other even further.

> "Using a condom to not get a disease is a scam, a diversion from the real disease. The real disease is 'energy transference.' Even if you have protected sexual intercourse, you are not protected at all. Energy knows neither time nor space, it can penetrate all things"

If you think about it, if you have to use a condom to be safe, it means that you don't trust the person you are engaging sexually with. If you don't trust that person, then why do you even engage with that person? Because your lower mind says so - lust. Unless you use a condom so that she (or you if you are a woman reading this) doesn't get pregnant.

Q-*If you don't want her to get pregnant, why do you want to have sex with her?*

A-*Because you want to have pleasure, meaning you are using each others' bodies as objects.*

Sex (including orgasm) is the forbidden fruit. Look at our society where people are multiplying like rabbits. There is no problem if two awakened healthy people procreate where they will raise children to be free, happy, rebels and conscious/self-aware. The problem is that children in grown up bodies have children of their own. Many mothers end up having to even prostitute (not necessarily in the streets) themselves to provide food for their child/children. Isn't that sad? Tame the monster that you are so that you reward yourself. You read the chapter KARMA=ACTION didn't you?

Using a condom has become a norm in our society. Using a condom implies that it is ok to have sex, as long as you use a condom, but what they don't tell you is to not waste the most creative power in the universe which is "sexual energy". The mainstream doctors are ignorant, most of them anyway. They advise patients what they've been taught in the mainstream schools, they put young people on hormone disruptor birth control pills which messes up women's hormones and eventually they end up having sex with the wrong person since the mind/emotions are in distress.

No matter how many partners you go with, you will eventually feel empty because you are missing the main ingredient which is LOVE. When you love someone and receive the same love back you see no flaws with each other. When you are in Love, your brain releases a substance called "Oxytocin." Oxytocin is associated with trust, sexual arousal and relationship building. This hormone is sometimes referred to as the "love hormone" or "cuddle chemical." Oxytocin levels also increase when you are hugging someone. I wonder why the *six-feet-apart* was implemented when the fake Covid was going on? Perhaps they didn't want people to be too close to each other. Were the controllers afraid of people hugging each other? All rhetorical questions. Oxytocin is an essential hormone for childbirth and lactation.

DO YOU WANT TO KNOW HOW BILLIONAIRES AND TRILLIONAIRES MAKE THEIR MONEY?

They practice the universal law of manifestation and by also not wasting their sexual energy. For them to achieve that, they must also convince you to waste your sexual energy through sex, orgasm, masturbation, ejaculation. All these drain you, weaken your mind and you become an obedient citizen and a consumerist that enriches the billionaires even further.

I was a big consumerist until a few years ago. Not anymore, the billionaires are not getting anything from me. Well, they are getting the cut from selling this book. But in this case they deserve it, they print the book, they deal with delivery and any other potential problem. I only post the manuscript file on Amazon. I wasn't talking about this, I was talking about the billions of people that buy cars, brand clothing, all sorts of technological gadgets and many other nonsense objects that don't make them happy, instead it keeps them buying every time new gadgets get released for sale.

He who has zero dollars, is richer than he who pays something in monthly payments. I am talking about the regular people that work just to survive. I have seen people that earn a minimum wage using a $1000 cellphone. Why? Addiction, disease, that's why. If what you have/use/wear is still working, then there is no need to purchase a newer version of it. Another reason why people get the newest thing is because they don't want to be left out, they want to have what their friends have.

This proves that people don't know their own power, they value more what others think of them. It is impossible to be someone else. Everyone else is taken, everyone is unique. Don't be a copy, be original. When you die, all that will be worthy to your children is the knowledge that you give them and not how much money or materialistic belongings you leave to them. Have you ever enjoyed peace in the sun by yourself at one point in life? Everyone has. You didn't have to pay for that. **All the good things that makes you truly feel good are free**. Anything that you buy, will not last. Well, you bought/purchased this book, but this book is about knowledge and knowledge is not happiness. Knowledge is good but it must be consumed to lead you to happiness. When people love and care about one another, then there will not be any need for books. Books exist because society has been struggling for far too long. By universal common sense, when you learn something that you know will benefit the world, you are morally obligated to share the information.

For example, if this book is useful to you, share it with others. In this book I mentioned other author's books. You or the other people you'll share this book with (online or offline) will be exposed to more knowledge by reading the books of the other authors mentioned here. The point is that we must help each other in anyway we can for a better future for our children.

In *The Internal Dragon: The Art of Self-Mastery* by J.J., the author says this about chastity:

"Chastity, therefore, is both a discipline and a state of being. It purifies the astral body, enabling the soul to resonate with the frequency of the white dragon consciousness. This consciousness in not merely an abstract ideal but a living reality within the astral light, a force that empowers the soul to transcend the lower dimensions of the titanic existence and embrace the infinite. In this state, the initiate achieves gnosis – not through external knowledge but through an inward experience that arises when the soul, body, and spirit are aligned"

```
"He who has a garden and a library is the wealthiest
person." - Cicero
```

```
CHASTITY=IMMORTALITY. POLYGAMY=DEATH. BOTH ARE POISONS
OR CURES. DEPENDING ON KNOWLEDGE OF YOURSELF AND
WHETHER YOU THINK THAT TIME EXISTS OR NOT.
```

SACRED INTIMACY – INTO ME SEE

14 Nobody can complete you. You can only find completion within yourself. The purpose of mating (relationship) with someone, is to share your completeness. No such thing as *'the other half'*. Well, if you cut an apple in half and give one half to your friend, he or she has the other half. But you are not an apple, are you? You are a living conscious sentient being, you are full, complete, you are whole. Unless you realize this, you'll always chase a fictional "the other half". The best relationship you can have is the one with yourself. You must realize and live in sacred intimacy with yourself first before you attract those that will compliment (not complete) you.

In the movie "Rocky 3", when Rocky told his coach that he couldn't beat the opponent, among other things, Rocky's trainer Micky told Rocky that he got civilized, that's what happened. By "civilized" he meant that he got married, had a child and became a part of the herd mentality/society. Before Rocky had a child, he was strong as a bull. When he became a family man, he did not have that strength in his heart to really fight anymore. The point is that Rocky had lost that intimacy that he had with his true self, with who he truly was, he had become civilized. A man's legs become weak by a woman, meaning that a man loses his mind when he satisfies his base desires. At one point in this movie or in the previous one, in Rocky 2, Rocky's wife told him to not fight anymore. Fighting is what Rocky was good at. Then Rocky told her:

> "I never asked you to stop being a woman so please
> don't ask me to not be a man".

This proves that when men are themselves they can be very strong, when men become feminized they lose themselves. It doesn't mean that a man has to stay single but if he is with someone, then she must allow his masculinity to shine. After all, a woman is designed to mate with a masculine man. But societal customs/rules pressure women to get married and have children before or after their time is done.

For example, many women chase a career, which is an illusion by the way. Eventually, these women decide to settle and have a family/children. Many of these women are in their 40s or 50s. Their prime time is gone, their biological body is not as suitable to have children as it was in their 20s and early 30s. And because these women feel like they're running out of time, they rush and get together with the wrong person. To have children, one must undo all the damage from the poisons of the past before bringing a child to this world. Do not let anyone or anything to pressure you into having children. If you are late, then live with it, you'll have more chances in the next life or perhaps this is your last incarnation in a 3D reality.

Eventually women leave men that become weak. Women are designed to mate with strong intelligent men. Even if she makes a mistake of mating with a weak man, she will eventually be looking for the right one, no matter how long it takes. It is by design. Just as a man is designed to protect women and will mate with a woman that honors her divine feminine role.

Men and women complement each other, neither is better or worse. In our society many men and women put down each other, they have been conditioned to compare and compete, this causes them to operate in a low vibrational mind state. The only way to balance is in the union of the divine masculine and feminine beings. Otherwise balance cannot be reached.

UNION - MARRIAGE

Besides the legal marriage between a woman and a man which is just a contract with the state, there are other forms of marriages such as the ones mentioned below.

➤ If you are a frequent porn (or any online sexualization accounts) user/consumer or death, then you are married to lust.

➤ If you are an avid sports viewer, then you are married to external distractions.

➤ If you like spending money on things that don't fulfill your soul, then you are married to materialism.

➤ If you invest too much time in *movies or tv shows, or video games, you are married to technology/screens, artificial intelligence that benefits the inventors of those technologies and not you. *Speaking of movies, I was watching a movie on YouTube with my husband. It was just a regular movie. A few times when it showed a woman in a bathing suit, the skin on the outside of the bottom area and the side part of the breast were blurred out by whoever uploaded the movie.

I have seen the same in other movies, not just blurring out the skin but also muting certain words. What this tells me is that the system has weakened people, is teaching people to censor even basic things. And yet, internet is loaded with porn, pedophilia and many more gruesome and immoral things. The need for money, for clicks, for traffic to their YouTube channels, has cornered many people's minds. People have become so weak that even when you constructively criticize them, they call you names such as: judgemental, rude, not nice etc.

All the above four points are part of the _bread and circuses_ deception.

BREAD AND CIRCUSES

This term refers to the potential of spectator sports and mass spectacles to divert populations or factions of a population away from the weightier business of politics and society, and to entertain them with amusement and physical contests. This term can also be applied to Television and social media since these two are controlled by politics and mega corporations that want people to be distracted and not think for themselves. So pretty much porn, sports, materialism etc., are simply superficial appeasements.

In ancient Rome this term was used to describe an Emperor's policy of providing food and entertainment to the people in order to keep them happy and content. This tactic was used to keep the people from rebelling against the government. Even today they apply the same tactics to keep people happy (happy=distraction) without actually addressing people's needs or solving their problems. This phrase suggests that if people were given food (bread) they would not care about anything else, this way they would be happy to remain under the rule of the ruling class.

> Bread and circuses means food and entertainment. To
> keep the belly full and the mind busy with nonsense.

In those times both rich and poor would flock to see gladiator games and chariot races held in large public arenas such as the Colosseum. By the way The Colosseum in Rome is beautiful, I have been there and I suggest you visit Rome one day. To this day the same scheme has been played on people, in the present sports, materialism and mega stores loaded with unlimited quantities and varieties of foods and drinks, which by the way most of these products are poison, unhealthy for human consumption. You can say that Rome was never demolished, it is still thriving to this day under a different name, U.S.A. as ROME 2.0. If people don't awaken for real, then ROME 3.0 will be implemented.

Most couples don't have intimacy with each other anymore. Most couples want to gain something out of each other. In the case of men, they mostly want sex, and since they are being controlled by their sexual urges, their brain is fried and they act like children. A woman needs a grown up man and not a child that misses his momma. In the case of women, many of them use men for money, materialistic things, vacation, etc. This mindset is a poison planted by movies, especially cartoons. The mind of someone can be manipulated since a young age. Nowadays, most people have no clue what intimacy means. They don't know what real love means. They don't know themselves.

THE FIRST STEP TO KNOW WHAT LOVE OR INTIMACY MEANS, IS
TO KNOW YOURSELF. THE REAL SELF AND NOT THE ONE
SOCIETY CONDITIONED YOU TO THINK YOU ARE.

GROUNDING – POSITIVE/NEGATIVE
To ground yourself you should walk barefoot on the grass or soil, eat lots of fruit, do gardening without gloves, sit under the tree, hug a tree, talk to a tree, take Sun baths, Moon baths, walk in parks, in the forest, feed the birds, keep flowers at home and take care of them, breathe deep a few times with your eyes closed while barefoot on the soil or grass, jump for a minute on a trampoline every day. These will help you ground and reconnect with yourself. When you reconnect

with yourself you will glow and attract the opposite gender if you are balanced energetically, when both your feminine and masculine energies operate in coherence.

Here are some of the grounding benefits:

(1) Grounding improves quality of sleep and feelings of restfulness upon waking up.
(2) Grounding reduces muscle stiffness and soreness, it also reduces chronic pain.
(3) It normalizes secretion of the stress hormone cortisol.
(4) It reduces stress and balances your autonomic nervous system.
(5) It reduces the severity of the inflammatory response after intense workouts. When you ground yourself, your heart rate variability gets raised and your wound healing speeds up. Your mood improves, your blood gets thinner and also the structure of the water in your cells increases.

The *Woods Resort* stated, the Earth is full of wonderful and potent energy and when there is barefoot contact, free electrons from the Earth can be absorbed by our body. This energy can nourish your body, mind, and soul. Walking barefoot on the grass is an effective way to improve eyesight naturally.

There are points under the feet to which the eye-nerve system is attached. According to reflexology, applying pressure to those points can energize the eyes. Looking at green also relaxes your eye muscles.

In her book *The Complete guide to Chakras*, April Pfender stated, "*The hands and feet have incredibly powerful gateways that greatly impact your entire physical body and energetic system. Home to thousands of nerve endings, temperature and pressure sensors, and meridian lines, these small portals also contain a number of secondary chakras that allow energy to release from the body.*"

She stated in reflexology, pressure is applied to specific points on the hands and feet to clear "Chi", or vital energy, cleansing the corresponding organs and parts of the body. The pressure sensors in these areas directly link to zones on the body and, when stimulated, create waves of relaxation and detoxification that affect the intended areas.

Reflexology is used to prevent disease, remove energetic blockages, reduce pain and inflammation as stated above, improve health and well-being, and enhance vitality. Evidence suggests that the practice of reflexology dates back to the ancient Egyptians as well as Chinese medicine.

DECREE OF CLEANSING YOUR AURA

Practice mentally this decree before meditating, when you wake up or anywhere or any time you feel heavy of thoughts or concerns or anything that doesn't align with love/divinity. When you say your name, say the full name that you were given at birth.

```
I (insert your name) ask that every negative
energetic work, aggressors and entities not coming
from the Light, be addressed to my human being, or
any member of my family. If you (you are directing
your words at the entity) are here with a loving
intention, then you are welcomed to guide me in my
spiritual journey. Otherwise, if your intention is
to harm or manipulate my consciousness in anyway to
my disadvantage, then you must immediately leave.
```

Say your real name, the one parents gave you at birth because that's the sound that was anchored in the Akashic Records/Book of Life when you were born. By the universal law, any spiritual entity has to obey to yours or anyone else's command. You are your own God, you decide who does or does not communicate with you. Do not allow anyone to manipulate you into thinking that you do not have power. You have free will and you have to exercise it when any situation requires it to.

When you awaken, it's difficult to find another one like you. It is easy to find an asleep one that will drown you in shallowness, but very difficult to find an awakened one because it requires to dive deep in the ocean/within.

SPIRITUAL EGO - NPC

15 Allow me to teach you* how to think, instead of what to think. Here is a description of what I mean: I am an NPC in your world that exists only in your mind. If you like to drink alcohol/liquor, take drugs, watch sports to be distracted, vote for politicians etc., you are an NPC in my world, just as I am an NPC to you if I say, think or do many things differently than you. In this case we are not part of each other's inner world. We are not main actors; we are back drop players in each other's lives. In this description that I gave you, me being an NPC in your world and vice versa is not bad. It is normal that anyone is their own main actor in their own main movie/life path and it's how it should be. If I were to be condescending, looking down on you because you don't think like me, then that would make me an arrogant person which I am not of course. I am no better than you and you are no better than me.

We all are on the same train track/journey. It's just that some of us are ahead, and some others are stopping at the train stops to look around which eventually everyone will be on the train to the destination. Everyone is in their life where they are supposed to be. You may ask: If that's true that everyone is where they need to be, then why did I write this book? I wrote it for one main purpose, to help people not stop their momentum, and not push you faster than you can go. If a child/baby can only walk for now, you cannot make him run if his body structure is soft and only capable of walking.

The same applies to people as far as knowledge goes. In the case of this book, I am passing you the stick or the torch. Picture yourself in the middle of a deep muddy puddle, I pass you a stick so that I can help you get out of it. If you want to still stay in the hole, that's fine. I am here so you don't fall deeper in the hole. As for getting out of it, that is up to each individual. The same thing applies when others pass me the stick so that I do not sink in the hole that I am. In this metaphor the "hole" means limited knowledge and understanding. If you know 5 more things than me or if I know 1000 more things than you, it makes no difference because there are a trillion (actually unlimited) of things to know. The point is that the only reason to compare with someone else is for the purpose of inspiration, to the point that you get empowered by someone else's achievements and you are happy for them. Do not be envious of others, you'll only harm yourself.

Teach you – *I hope you didn't take this the wrong way. What I meant is to allow me to show you a different way on how to deal with things/ people. You may be reading this book, but you are also teaching me. I had to think and reflect on many subjects so that I could write this book for you. At the same time, I wrote it for myself thanks to you, since indirectly you taught me how to think deeper.*

When you converse with someone, do not have expectations, or else your experience will be limited, you'll be disappointed that they will not say things that align with what you know/believe and then you will reject them, or they will reject you. You both lose. Unless the conversation ends up in arguing, then you move away. In the past I have learned a lot of things from people that I thought knew much less than me. You can learn from anyone and anything. It is true that some people may be in a totally different frequency to yours. It doesn't make you better than them.

10 or 20 years ago you too were on a different frequency. How would you feel if people called you an NPC 10 or 20 years ago, and vice versa. If you can help someone, please do so. If not, then guide them to others that may help them. Not everyone can be a teacher. My husband plays piano, he is very good at it, but he gets aggravated/ mad when he teaches. Different people express themselves in their own way. I wrote this book, I express myself freely, but it doesn't mean that I would be very patient if you and I were face to face talking. Just as the piano example, you may be good at something but you may not be so good at teaching what you're good at. Do not look down on people that know and understand less than you. You too know and understand less than other people that are on a higher level. No amount of knowledge can make up for apathy toward your fellow human brothers and sisters. No amount of good shading (speaking of drawing/art) can make up for wrong proportions of whatever it is that you are drawing or painting.

You are controlled by your EGO:

When you feel superior to others, you feel self righteous.

When you think you are more spiritual than others.

When you feel people should think and be like you.

When you believe you know it all.

When you compare yourself to others, which breeds jealousy.

If you feel superior to others you have EGO issues, because you identify with a corrupted identity of yourself that you have created. You think you know it all. I'll tell you a little secret. "we know nothing." None of us know anything. Apply this (remind yourself of this phrase) daily and you will always learn more and help others. Since you have created this fictional identity of yourself as being superior to others, you refuse to learn from anyone, because the EGO is threatened if you allow yourself to listen to reason. You can also develop jealousy/envy when someone knows/says something that you didn't, so the jealousy creates a thicker wall between what you know and what needs to be known. You will tend to become condescending without realizing that at one point you were in that situation where you needed someone to give you a hand.

You expect others to be like you and think like you. I have news for you, nobody has to think like you, and you don't have to think like anyone else either. To learn more you must allow others to express themselves and say what they have to say, they don't have to agree with you. If someone doesn't agree with you, it doesn't mean that what you say/think is wrong. It just means that you are in a different state of knowledge and understanding, but not better than them. Everyone is already whole. The work you have to do on yourself to realize the wholeness, is like a sculptor that chisels away the pieces of the rock, when the sculptor is done chiselling, then the bust/person appears. It was always there buried deep within the rock (ocean of separation, self-made identities, opinion, ideologies).

This whole concept of NPCs is simply a justification for people to treat others badly. This is **SP** {Spiritual Ego} The individual "decided" that THEY are real and then spends the rest of their life deciding for the rest of humanity who deserves respect and who deserves to be treated like a department store mannequin.

Calling someone an NPC in a condescending way is the greatest height of arrogance and entitlement; it dehumanizes those that are fragile and need help. The individual deserves better. Spiritual ego causes one to lose respect. Many so-called spiritual inclined people justify every sort of undivine destructive behavior we see in the world today. This is not the behavior of someone who is spiritually self-aware. Being condescending to someone that you think is lesser than you is the attitude of an adult child that has grown only in age, never developed any sort of empathy, and has a very fragile grip on reality.

People who have this concert of NPCs, are ego soaked and have no idea what a true spiritual path is. Unless the term NPC is used to describe the role of someone in your life, just as you are an NPC in someone else's reality/life. I have witnessed a lot of talk in recent years about "NPCs" or what's called "non-player characters" and it's alarming. The amount of people that have no clue to what's really going on, calling others NPCs. Everyone has a role to play. For example: Thanks to those that got vaccinated, which to you may be NPCs, you got exposed to an unlimited amount of knowledge about many things. A lot of truthers created truth/knowledge accounts online posting researched information about the vaccines or the government etc. So, indirectly the vaccinated ones helped you. From the darkness, the light is shining from within this world. If the vaccination or Covid didn't happen, people would continue living a mundane, boring, worrying, and fearful life. The point is that all of us had to burn our hands so we could realize that the fire burns.

The concept of an "NPC" is a tool used to elevate the ego...to make one think you are the "Lead Actor" and "NPCs" are soulless characters. Dolores Cannon talks about the terms "Backdrop People" or NPCs. The concept that Dolores Cannon was trying to explain was that your life is YOUR PLAY. Other people you interact with may be "backdrop" people in the play of your life. It doesn't mean they don't have souls, it just means they are not "lead players" in your life. You too are a "backdrop player" in the role of someone else's life, does that mean you are an "NPC" with no soul?

The Earth is a place where there are multiple "plays" going on at the same time, like different channels with different tv shows/Radio channels playing. Everyone is part of the whole. Do not fall into the mind control trap that one person, one race, one ethnicity or one gender is any better than the other. The trap is designed to keep us fighting against each other instead of loving and caring about one another. We are ALL divine beings and not any single one of us is better than the other. You are responsible for your life, your choices and the path you take. This NPC term is blown out of proportion. Those that have developed a spiritual ego need to somehow feel special when compared to others.

NPC's or "back drop" people are just people that have nothing to do with your soul's journey. Just like when you walk by people on the street, you pass by random people that you do not interact with at all. Are they NPCs? Well, it depends on how you define the term NPC, from a critical thinking self-aware mindset or through a level of spiritual ego. That doesn't make them soulless or lesser than you. They too are real, just like you, they have a soul and a journey of their own that they are focusing on, even though from your point of view they look like zombies/sheep to you. What would Manly P. Hall, Alan Watts, Rene Descartes, Socrates, Plato etc. think of you, that you are a zombie/Npc? Do you see how it works? We are backdrop people/ NPC's in someone else's life.

The only difference is that there are people that are more connected and people who aren't but even that is not accurate because we are all at different stages of evolution/ awakening. We are all going in the same direction, some are further along on the journey and some are not, but we are all on the same trip. Some souls who we would call NPCs based on their actions are incredible beings, and for many various reasons, they are asleep and passive. It would be wise for us to never judge (in a condescending way) a soul, and to never look up or down upon another soul, for we are all one.

> Have you ever planted vegetable seeds in the ground? They don't all sprout at the same time. Sometimes the seeds that are slow to sprout, are building stronger roots, and when they sprout they grow faster, bigger and healthier.

I am not vaccinated, some of the people that I know are vaccinated and some others are not. Half of the vaccinated ones I know are much smarter than some of the unvaccinated ones. These ones were pressured by their work or parents. It is not an excuse, because everyone is responsible for their own actions, but getting vaccinated was a wake-up call for these ones I'm talking about and for many others in the world. I also know a fair amount of unvaccinated people that are not intelligent at all, some of these people call the vaccinated ones NPCs. You can guess who's the intelligent one in this case. Regardless, everyone has their own wake-up call.

I recommend you watch the movie Free Guy. Even the NPCS can evolve. You just have to break the loop! We are all NPCs believing we are not. It's amazing to see everyone assuming that THEY are a "player" in an "avatar". Ego makes someone think they are above others. Everything you believe or don't believe becomes your reality. All you need is the belief that you're not an NPC, and voila, you're not, according to you. If everyone is an NPC, there aren't any NPCs at all... there's nothing to compare to. So, in a sense we're agreeing with each other.

REAL NPC

A real NPC will always protect and support the programming and they will do whatever they are told by who they perceive to be the authorities that know what is best for them. This applies to whomever refuses to wake up or whomever is an actual NPC, with their empathy gene suppressed. They're not capable of using critical thinking skills and their programming is so deep that they're usually not capable of rebelling against their own programmers and will defend them at all cost. Cognitive dissonance is the major defect or program of an NPC. When you have spiritual intuition you are equipped with the vital tool and a weapon against the dark forces/ magicians that hold humanity captive and use people as their energy supply.

We live in holographic manifestations that become alive through people's actions, emotions, feelings, and people who only spend short bursts of time into your life. I don't prescribe to this NPC consciousness - it's a pretty small pendulum and it's mostly based off of binary universe laws - which isn't our base universe, but a fake matrix created to keep us trapped in a delusion and delirium. The NPC reality exists, anything you can imagine you can create. It doesn't mean this low consciousness reality needs to be yours.

This NPC delirium is also part of the fake New Age people that justify their right to be saved while others are left behind by stating they are the 144,000 chosen ones and everyone else is an NPC. This just seems like a natural progression that the mind goes through by trying to balance itself with the fake New Age/ Chrystic ideologies spewed by supposed light workers, those that write and say the term "light and love" non-stop. These fake so-called light workers that refuse to face the darkness of their soul, clearly want the world to burn but also want to save it.

NPCs only affect you if you are living daily in the binary universe/ separation mindset. If you are still in that bleed through, where the world is a "computer program" then you will have to deal with all sorts of different frequencies or realities. NPCs only affect or bother you if you are still running around in matrices founded in the binary universe. If you are still in that bleed through, where the world is a "computer program" then yeah- you're going to believe this. I've seen people who have bled through- who you can't see their souls and what not, I've seen a lot of things- but who is really feeding that reality? Not the NPCs many claim to exist. They can't. They have no energy to contribute to their own existence

So, from what I know, an NPC is a "nonplayable character." Someone who lacks thinking for themselves. So, you are the main character in your life and your choices. Once you open your eyes up to accountability, you can help get yourself away from having others think for you. This will help you get to the enlightening better and smoother.

For now many are NPCs or Backdrop people, but I do believe some are less aware than others. These people are no more and no less than anyone else with their own realities. The awareness also involves self control, if the animal in you is the one holding the wheel and you just do whatever, you are essentially not playing the character, not being an individual. When pure animal instincts overtake the mind, you become one with the DIVINE (on a basic level), therefore "Non-Playable-Character" because as humans we strive to carve out our own ways instead of relying on our animalistic nature.

You are an NPC if you go with the flow of this fake made-up finite Matrix because you haven't deviated from the fake prison path. You must get off and carve your own path where you are the one that decides how your life goes, a life where whatever it is that you do, helps the world, people and the whole ecosystem.

People who are still stuck in this system's web of lies are everywhere. They interact and listen to their program full of lies, control and manipulation. Their comfort slowly sucks the life out of their empathetic supplies. The dark magicians are looking and praying to destroy their light bodies, they are in a war with our spirits, our divine consciousness. Protect yourself with the white or golden light. The Light is death to them.

These dark magicians were officially called Archons but yes they are beings whose DNA is too convoluted for them to experience "awakening". These Archons have no empathy, they have not evolved past their reptilian brains. They are among us, they have families, they have also reincarnated into families of light. In many families you'll find out that an Archon (or real NPC) is in a family of benevolent parents, while in other families benevolent children are the black sheep of the family surrounded by NPC parents and siblings.

Anytime you bring up the topic of importance these NPCs will default to their programming which is to shut you down through their cognitive dissonance or make you look like a fool so you shut the conversation down. Even if you have all the facts and evidence to support an important topic/subject, to them won't matter. They operate on a different frequency than you. Just like TV channels exist in the same box/tv, but they cannot hear/see each other. The same applies to you where you can be face to face with an actual NPC where both of you are on a totally different frequency. It's like living worlds apart, no matter how close or loud you are with your common sense and educated opinions on any given topic.

Look at the artwork (Religion/ Spirituality/ Consciousess). A lot of so called spiritually awakened people make fun of religious people. Religious people, alcoholics, liars, boasters, killers and everyone else is a spiritual person. We all are spirits. It's that different people are at a different level of awareness. Divine Consciousness is everywhere, in people, plants, air, oceans, thoughts, feelings etc. We are all ONE, period. Transcend duality and watch how you will then decide every step of the way and think for yourself and make righteous conscious choices in life.

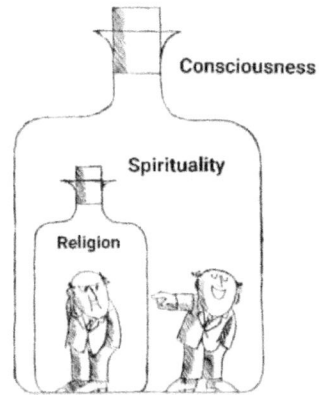

If you are someone that makes fun of another person that is still asleep comparing (according to you) it to your level of awareness, know that you too are still asleep compared to other people/beings that know and understand much more that you could ever learn and understand in this lifetime.

You should help others get up and not knock them down even further then they have been knocked by the system. If you make fun of someone because you know a thing or two more than them, is like holding the lit light bulb away from them in the pitch-dark forest instead of pointing the light so they can find the way. Never forget that what goes around comes around, you reap what you sow, what you cause will have an effect.

Alcohol and *sex among other things can kill your soul. Well, not literally kill and a soul can never truly die, but confuse it, suppress it, make it feel defeated. Know that your soul houses your physical body and not the other way around so anything good or bad that you do to your body, it's like doing it to your soul too. You are the body and the soul at the same time. In this realm, your soul cannot exist without your body and your body cannot exist without a soul. Unless we are speaking of actual NPCs A.I.

*sex - Any sexual interaction that is not *complete between masculine and feminine energies.
*complete - When the energy between the woman and the man circulates inside, without dissipating externally. Complete is when the men doesn't ejaculate, when the woman and the man have completed the battery circle/effect, where they recharge each other as opposed to drain one another and that is *white tantric sex*. Any other kinds of sex will age you and you'll die faster.

> HUMBLE YOURSELF DAILY BY SAYING: I KNOW NOTHING AND THAT I AM NOBODY.

SPIRITUAL FALSE LIGHT

16 There is NEW AGE but there is also FAKE New Age. Fake light/information has been injected in books, social media, schools etc. In recent years you must have heard, read from people that everything is an experience, whether it is suffering or joy. There are conscious but also unconscious experiences. Many people have this belief that there is no such thing as right or wrong. This is false teaching; it is poison for the mind. What this belief does is, makes a person passive for all the injustice that one or a group of people do in the world.

Of course, there is such a thing as right or wrong. Is it right to take the life of another human being, or is it wrong? Would you kill your own child? Would you kill a random stranger? In the grand scheme of things, your child is not any more important than a stranger is. On a spiritual atomic, energetic level we all are made in the image of the ALL, or God if you prefer to use this term, therefore, your child is the stranger, the stranger is your child, your friend, or anyone else for that matter.

As far as killing goes, there is one exception, when it's about defending yourself. It is a universal divine law which nobody has the right to take your life away. You have no right to take anyone else's life away unless it for self-defence. If anyone threatens to take your life away, they have lost their right to live, so you have absolutely every reason to defend yourself. A lot of people die in wars, genocides have happened for a long time. Many people do nothing about it, they think: *"What can we do, we have no power"*.

Evil entities have existed for a very long time, they still exist because they have manipulated people to be passive, to not rebel when fellow brothers and sisters are getting killed left and right for all kinds of reasons. A good-hearted rebellious person is someone who fights for freedom even when they are not suffering. When you rebel against tyranny because of seeing others suffering, you deserve respect. Many people try to defend themselves when something happens to them, that's reactionary fighting.

A while back I used to follow a woman on Instagram. She used to post esoteric knowledge. A lot of what she posted was good. The false light (poison, misinformation, conditioning) has infected many truthers. I commented something about people needing to defend against tyranny and I got a reply from her saying among other things that *"there is no such a thing as right or wrong"*. That moment was the moment I knew her mind was hijacked by the false light. Another commenter replied to her with: *"So if someone kills or rapes your child is it okay?"* Well, she didn't answer, only a fool would defend suffering, slaughter, raping, killing etc.

The School And The Prison Life Analogy
The Earth was meant to be a school and not a prison. There is a big difference between struggling and suffering. After a rainy day, you enjoy the Sun more. I'll try to explain this through an analogy.

When it rains and you go out, you'll just get wet and may feel annoyed by the rain. After the rain stops, the clouds disappear, the Sun appears and you'll feel better. Now, Imagine if the rain droplets were little stones. What if instead of the stones, bricks fell from the sky?

Rain = Annoyance
Little rocks = Struggling
Bricks = Suffering

If bricks fell on you, you will either be dead or so hurt that you wouldn't even pay attention to the Sun after. The same applies to our life. Many people are suffering so much mentally, physically and spiritually that when knowledge/truth is presented to them, they are too passive and defeated to do something about improving their lives. The rain can be seen as "the school", metaphorically speaking, where you will use an umbrella next time. In the little rocks analogy, you would answer it by staying inside so you won't get hurt at all. When the bricks fall, well, that's like already having one foot 6 feet under (meaning almost dead). Do not allow yourself to end up in a situation where your life could be forfeited.

Before going out of the house check the weather (School). Which means that before you deal with the external environment (prison), make sure that your mind is clear, your emotions are under control and your spiritual path is in your field of view. Otherwise, your own mind can be the most deadly prison. Sometimes (actually most of the time) a seed can grow in the dark much faster and stronger.

When you are distracted by "supposed *knowers*" you forget your own mission and you end up getting lost in the opinions of others. Even though other people's opinions are truths to them, you must find your own truth. You can learn from your mistakes just as much as you can learn from others. Just be careful that you don't go beyond that fine line where you get sucked in the external world and forget the one within.

In this world you have to deal with people's non genuine intentions but also with your own false light, assuming what you think you are and who you think you are is a result of external conditioning. No matter how many good and intelligent genuine people you meet in life, in the end you have to forge your own path. Different people have different strengths and weaknesses. Someone else's strength may compel you to feel weak if you do not know your own strength. Someone else's weakness can suck you into their world and get you to become even weaker. But if you have a clear mind and become an observer without getting emotionally engaged in situations that you have no control of, then both the situations of people's strengths and weaknesses will help you become stronger than what you already are.

WHEN YOU LEARN THAT YOU CAN ONLY CONTROL
YOUR OWN THOUGHTS, WORDS AND ACTIONS,
YOU'LL REACH A NEW LEVEL OF FREEDOM.

GOD IS EVERYWHERE AND NOWHERE

17 What/who do you think God is, a person, or an unseen energy? To find God, you have to revert one's mind back to God. That depends on which path you are on, the one where you are looking for God or the one where you realize that God is in you and not out there. Even though in this chapter you will read that God is everywhere, in your reality God is only within yourself, although on a frequency level God is everywhere.

One simply has to remember God (frequency). Society has distorted our perceptions since birth, so it's up to ourselves to reverse indoctrination and unlearn belief systems so that the collective consciousness may return to KNOWING SOURCE and not just "believing" in an unseen force/power. Our very essence has the experience of GOD within us but we're over stimulated with illusions of physical reality. If you're searching for the truth outside of yourself, you will never find it. GO WITHIN.

There is nothing but Source and Source Creative Intelligence, Source Power. Within is all we need for true peace. God is all that is, the greatest force of energy and love. *"Society has distorted our perceptions since birth"*. It is not simply a "change your thoughts and you will see God" thing. Those perceptions have been changed by the storing of tension inside of us. That tension pulls us out of balance and literally changes our physical ability to see different perspectives. As within, so without.

When we physically cannot see different perspectives, then we mentally can't see different perspectives. To change that, we need to release that tension, that past programming. We got the answers in ourselves and many don't know that this already happened with an intention of God creation. We have to simply understand that and accept that fact this is answer to the ONE (you are the One, created in the image of the GREAT ONE), the question is what is love? Don't do unto others what you don't want to do to be done onto yourself. There is no God outside of you in the sky. All humans are a collective of God being connected to It.

God is everything that exists in space and form, universal cosmic consciousness and absolute sentient power. We are the microcosm of the macrocosm. God source divine energy is consciousness, consciousness is energy so everything is energy, your original being, your soul is energy the same as light/love, vibration/frequency. You are not the body (check the chapter "*I THINK, THEREFORE I AM*". The spiritual soul and everlasting divine energy is a sparkle from God source divine energy, you are the universe.

The word God means different things to different people. Be careful when you say "God". To many people, God means the God being who made earth and everything in it. Do you think that there is only the Earth and nothing else? Have you ever been beyond the 60th parallel? You will be shot down; the Shadow Government don't want you to know what's in Antarctica and beyond. Let alone seeking to go in the supposed North Pole a.k.a. the Center Pole.

This applies to those that think/believe that God is a person/being. God and Satan are the same thing. For one (God) to be defined, the opposite (Devil or Satan) must exist. God or Satan personified entities are concepts seeded in people's minds to keep them away from going within. The "Supreme Creator/God" or "Satan" if you wish to use these terms, are "frequencies" that exist within you. You decide which frequency you align to, the truth or the lie, the light or the darkness, the good or the evil.

What really is God?
God is consciousness, (not a creator as in a physical man up in the sky). When I use the word "God" I describe the Supreme Creator/ Consciousness, the energy that permeates everything and everyone, so don't get hung up on the word. God is the source of creation itself." IT " (not he or she). IT is not independent of you. It is the totality of everything. So, when I call myself (when you realize that God is hidden within you) "God" I Am not talking about my personal self. I AM talking about the expression of the God self that rests inside of me, the " I AM ". The verb, the ENERGY, not the noun. Once you

think God is a noun, person, place or thing, you separate yourself from it and immediately become a limited human being. That's what separates the beLIEvers (organized religion) from the KNOWers (spirituality). Many people abuse the word "God". God is not a human, statue or any religion. The aether/electromagnetic pulse of energy that gives life and lives within all living things is what God is. If you think or want to believe that God is a person that watches over you at all times, that's fine. You are the creator of your reality.

You must tune and connect to IT (neither he or her, or both he and her). You need a transmitter to connect to God, that transmitter is called "the 3rd eye or the pineal gland". Satan or God are the same thing, these are frequencies within you. You must achieve balance: Ying-Yang, Positive-Negative, Good-Bad, Masculine-Feminine. People are too obsessed with God (the personification), and that is a type of fear, it is hidden disbelief. Only when you don't know yourself you'll resort to outside saviors.

The process of loving life is more important than the goal in meeting God. So, either you think God is a person waiting for you, meanwhile you lose by not living in the moment, or God is a frequency that is ever present, every moment where you are one with it. Relax your mind, start to live life as it is intended. Don't waste time in trying to find out who created us, we will never find out for as long as we don't learn how to take care and love each other. **Become ever more present, breathe, and feel.** Many people have problem with the word God as did I for a long time because I was associating the words God with religion. Depends on what or who you think God is. If you think that your savior is outside of yourself, is different than if you think that you are your own saviour. **The breath of the Great spirit, or the omnipotent God is within each one of us.** Whatever it is that you think the truth is, you are right. You have been given the free will and the ability to think for yourself. You decide how you create your own reality.

People give all kinds of excuses as to why things happen to them, they blame or worship an external personality to justify their actions. For as long as people refuse to take responsibility for their action, they will struggle mentally and emotionally. This paragraph is referring to the artwork (Steve/God).

God is the ABSOLUTE ONE, the ONE that is alive through everyone and everything.

The ALL ONE, the Omnipotent, The Omnipresent, the Absolute Intelligence that keeps everything glued together, the ONE that is nowhere and everywhere, the one that is nobody and everybody. You give your life meaning. All you have to do to realize the Creator/Creation is simply to pay attention to your breath. Breathe consciously and try to realize how magnificent you are. Start from your breathing, analyze each part of your body and then you should come to the great realization. The story of creation is a metaphor.

"**Adam** is an Atom. **Eve** is an Electron. The story is mythology based on life beginning with "Splitting the Atom", as electrons are the 'rib' of the Atom. **God** is the 'Good' of your higher mind, the Cerebrum. **Devil** is the 'Evil' of your lower mind, the Cerebellum. **Heaven** is your 'Head', the highest 'heaved' up place of your body and higher nature. **Hell** is your 'Heel', the lowest place of your body and lower nature. The **serpent** is electromagnetic energy. The **tree** is your spine. The **apple** is consciousness. **Kundalini** energy means activating your pineal gland; hence, conquering your dragon."

I love this metaphor (two babies in the womb) describing God/The ALL ONE being here, there, nowhere and everywhere.

TWO BABIES IN THE WOMB
In a mother's womb were two babies. One asked the other:
"Do you believe in life after delivery?"
The other replied, "Of course, there has to be something after delivery. Maybe we are here to prepare ourselves for what will be later."
"Nonsense", said the first baby. "There is no life after delivery. What kind of life would that be?"
The second one said: "I don't know, but there will be more light than here. Maybe we will walk with our legs and eat with our mouths. Maybe we will have other senses that we can't innerstand now."
The first one replied: "That is absurd. Walking is impossible. Eating with our mouths? Ridiculous! The umbilical cord supplies nutrition and everything we need but the umbilical cord is short. Life after delivery is to be logically excluded."

The second insisted, "Well, I think there is something and maybe it is different than it is here. Maybe we won't need this physical cord anymore."

The first baby replied: "Nonsense. And moreover, if there is life, then why has no one ever come back from there? Delivery is the end of life, and in the after-delivery, there is nothing but darkness, silence and oblivion. It takes us nowhere."

"Well, I don't know," said the second, "but certainly we will meet our Mother and she will take care of us"

The first replied, "Mother? You actually believe in a Mother? That's laughable. If a mother exists, then where is she now?"

The second said, "She is all around us. We are surrounded by Her. We are Her. It is in Her that we live. Without Her, this world would not and could not exist."

The first one said: "Well, I don't see Her, so it is only logical that She doesn't exist."

To which the second replied, "Sometimes, when you are in silence and focus and listen, you can perceive Her presence, and you can hear Her loving voice, calling down from above and from within."

———————————

Just as the babies in the womb couldn't see their creator, neither do we. The babies couldn't see a world outside of their womb, just as we cannot see a world beyond this system that we live in. The babies' story metaphor should stretch your imagination into thinking beyond of what is officially known. Atoms and electrons and protons are everywhere, in humans, animals, trees, plants, stones, waters, air which means that God, the one that permeates everything and everyone is everywhere and present at all times. It is up to you to realize and embrace this absolute truth, or to keep believing that God is somewhere out there.

God **created*** all and all is one so all is love, the highest vibration. Big bang (conception/zygote stage) split one into dark and light to experience the diversity.

Humans are born with the spark of love, but different places and consciousness scales between dark and light. The big bang I wrote is about the meeting of the spermatozoa with the egg which then results in the creation of life.

Created* - The word God before the word "created" implies that God is a person. This conflicts with the paragraph earlier that describes that God is a frequency and not a person. Unfortunately, not only that written language is the lowest form of communication (telepathy is the best way to communicate with zero misunderstanding), but religion or those that hijacked it have done a great damage by conditioning people that their savior is outside of themselves. So, I and I'm sure other authors have to describe "God" in many different ways since there are many people that define God in their own way.

To some, God is a bearded man up in the sky, to others, God is also Satan which is also true by having in mind that we are a creation based on duality where both good/God and evil/Satan exist in us. Technically, everyone is right, everyone has the power to realize the most simple truth of all, and yet billions of people find it very difficult to accept that we all are little Gods, or little Satans. Our daily actions prove it so.

Little Gods – We are created in the image of the Great Supreme Intelligence or God, but not as in us being little humans and God being a human but Big. No, we are energy/frequency, therefore we are part of the whole universe which is frequency. When we operate from our hearts, when we think for ourselves, when we live our lives in accordance with Divine Nature, we are Gods.

Little Satans – When we operate out of our lower mind, when we are controlled by carnal pleasures I.E. abusing our bodies with foods, drinks, sex, personal gain, being distracted with materialism, hurting each other, being envy/jealous, keeping grudge, gossiping about each other etc., we operate in disharmony, we feed the beast within, that beast is Satan. If you think Satan is somewhere out there, that's on you. Well, having in mind the "as above so below" term, there are higher beings out there, malevolent and benevolent ones. They exist to keep the balance. Who they are is none of our concern, our concern is to do good, be good, think for ourselves, help one another in any way we can. This is the only way to bring peace and balance in our lives. Until then, the world will be full of little Satans a.k.a. minions of the greater Satans that lurk in the DARKNESS.
Open your mind

The explanations that I'm writing about God/Satan, can be controversial to a closed-minded person. The definition of insanity is when you do the same thing over and over and expecting the same result. It won't happen, you must open your mind that perhaps there is more space (knowledge/truth) beyond the small dark room you've been living all your life.

Do you remember the metaphor of the two babies in the womb? Picture yourself living for 30 years in a room without windows or doors where all you know is the inside of the room. If you are curious to know and open your mind that maybe there is a world outside of the room, then you will discover new unlimited horizons. I hope the two metaphors are clear by now as to why it is important to be an open-minded person. You cannot grow by repeating what you know/understand and wanting to hear others say things that you want to hear. You learn from being poked by thorns (getting triggered), but only if you admit to not knowing anything and are willing to open your mind.

There are different dimensions and planes in existence, one reaches the highest and enlighten state which is the ultimate (The Supreme Creator) and the other leads to destruction and pain (Satan). Until you reach the highest plane, you will not have an understanding of the ALL (Quantum Field or Supreme God). I purposefully use different terms to describe the ALL/God because to many people the word God is ingrained in a way that keeps them enslaved to their own ignorance/thinking.

As the creator of all, the God as I know which is love, the love for self with all its flaws (technically there are no flaws but suppressed goodness), aim to light and shine were darkness dwells, the compassion with understanding and care for life on earth for all living beings without judgment and with unconditional love. Forgiveness rewards you when you see things for what they are and you are ready to change your life for the better without harming anyone, intentionally or unintentionally.

Bringing heaven on earth is for everyone and not just for the privileged ones. If you have little understanding of the pain, at the gate of your success in hoarding money and wealth for personal gain, you will begin to dive in the ocean of great pain that you will have to endure. The more you disregard humanity for personal gain, the harder the fall. You will become food for the dark forces causing more suffering which ripples out to others and beyond.

You are little God made in the image of the Great God/

One. Everything is energy, there are many different frequencies that vibrate at a different rate/speed. This difference in vibration is what causes you to look like a human, a cat like a cat, a tree like a tree etc. So, God is everywhere, in you, in animals, plant, birds, air, in everything seen and unseen. Look at yourself in the mirror, look at others, close your eyes and visualize anything beautiful and loving, anything that could benefit society. The Creator is everywhere and in everyone. This is what I know and this is what I will continue expressing anywhere I go and to anyone I meet. If you think that God is somewhere there, that is perfectly fine. You are the cause and the effect. We all choose ourselves through righteous thoughts, words and actions. In the book (page 243) To Be Reborn by Tamo A. Replica, the author has this to say about the so-called 144,000 chosen ones:

"Is the 144k our dormant DNA? When all of our DNA awakens, it allows us to utilize all aspects of who we truly are. The number 144 is a divine number [all numbers are divine, depending on the meaning that we attach to them]. Once the dormant DNA awakens in people, the whole world will awaken to the truth of who we really are. No such a thing as "junk DNA" as the mainstream scientists want us to believe. There is only dormant or suppressed and unrealized DNA".

"Your thymus gland has 144 Akenenic cells. These cells cannot die, these cells are immortal, including the first 8 cells of the beginning of life which are immortal. These cells are connected to the Divine Infinite Source, the All That Is. There are also 144k piezoelectric microcrystals inside your pineal gland. To embody higher consciousness, we must unblock/decalcify the pineal gland, the seat of the soul".

I AM YOU. YOU ARE ME. THE SOONER WE REALIZE THIS. THE SOONER WE BECOME FREE

DÉJÀ VU & TIME TRAVEL

18 Did you ever have a Dejavu moment? Pretty much everyone has had one at one point or another in time. When two parallel timelines converge with each other, you can have that feeling as if you've already experienced it before. There is an infinite number of potentials that all your parallel timelines could go, so depending on which timelines converge, is what you'll experience. You are a multidimensional being which means that a Dejavu moment can happen from a combination of past lifetimes, or timelines from higher or lower dimensions. A Dejavu moment can also happen when one of your future selves a.k.a. future potentials has gone back in time (not your physical body but your consciousness) and reincarnated in your past lives and you are reliving it again. Dreams trigger all potentials.

When you dream, you have access to all possible future or parallel potentials. Technically, in this realm we use the words/terms "past and future" because our dense physical body can exist in a linear time but your spirit is boundless. We live the same life over and over again but with tiny changes on a microcosmic scale. You can even imagine or foretell a future event that hasn't happened yet. That is one of countless potential future timelines. It will be what you focus your energy most on. Could Dejavu be a glitch in the Matrix, where there is only a limited number of programmed scenarios and eventually sooner or later you will run into one of them? Could your future or parallel self have clashed/converged with your present one?

When timeline shifts (to higher or lower frequency) Dejavu happens, but also possible that your higher self is showing you that you live in a reality that is not what you think it is. Déjà vu moments also happen because your auric field is fractured by deviant electromagnetic energies that you've been bombarded all life, from atomic bombs experiments that the governments do, from a lot of airplane flights and from electronic devices that you use daily.

All these fracture your electromagnetic field. And to protect yourself from the deviant attacks you must build an energetic cocoon mentally. On how to build this cocoon or a protective bubble of white light check the book *Rebuild yourself from within* by J.J & Tamo.

When your auric field is not fractured anymore, then you have no more **karmic debts***. Protecting yourself with this cocoon or bubble of white light is very important. You can visualize this cocoon in your mind anytime you don't feel healthy, or when you feel emotionally unsettled, so pretty much you can raise your vibrational field every time you wish so that you will not be enslaved by low vibrational frequencies.

karmic debts* - Quite a few people are confused as to what a karmic debt is. You do not owe anyone any debts except to yourself. There is only Cause and Effect. You reap what you sow - ACTION/ReACTION.

....

Your higher self is winking at *YOU*
through *DÉJÀ VU*
the feeling of having already experienced that *SITUATION*
where you are ready for any kind of *MANIFESTATION*

....

I'd say that Dejavu is seeing or feeling fragments of your past life but on a conscious state. But there is also an experiencing of past life memories through meditation in an unconscious state. Sometimes a dream you had at one point in your life can be manifested as Dejavu. I strongly suggest you journal your dreams and once in a while read what you dreamt so that you know if the dreams will trigger remembrance of important past events and/or foreshadowing of something important that you need to do in the future (one of the unlimited potentials). All the examples I mentioned are part of the ascension process. The Universe or the Creator or the Void, whatever you want to call it, always nudges you with light [information, intuition, knowledge, and insight].

It is up to you to pay attention to the messages. We all dream daily but most people just ignore the dreams and go on continuing their daily routine/mundane life. The after life, or the unseen world communicates with us all the time, we must not ignore it. Dejavu is also a hint to let you know the existence of re-incarnation.

Time travel has existed since the beginning of time. If you do not believe that time travel exists, it means that you think you are your body, it means that you identify in three-dimensional state of mind/reality. Your mind is boundless, the only thing that halts your mind from its full potential is your perception of self. I'm sure that in your mind you can recall moments of the past, or imagine what could happen in the future about specific situations. That is time travel, basic time travel of course.

You may think that's ridiculous. Look at the trillions of cells in your body, working in perfect synergy with your blood, skin, flesh, bones, your nervous system etc. This happens 24/7 and you (most people anyway) have no clue as to what's going on for them to exist and live. So, the same applies to your memories and imagination a.k.a. time travel. Based on your level, perhaps when you are done living this life, you will time travel 500 years ago, or in a different parallel timeline.

But because you have been conditioned by Hollywood, you think time travel as in your physical body going back in time. Although I think that is possible. Scientists have already managed to teleport particles from point A to point B, and this was decades ago. What about now? When you meditate properly, you can time travel, all of us time travel daily but we are too distracted with nonsense to realize it how magnificent of a creation that we are. Watch the movie **TIMECOP** with Jean-Claude-VAN DAMME.

Dreams are other realities, other dimensions that you live in. Dreams are a sneak peak to your multiverse self. Always journal your dreams. There is a good reason why you dream. Just make sure that you have your internet off while you are sleeping so that no astral parasitic entities tries to infiltrate your mental/astral body. This reality that you are in, is but a dream to your other selves from other realities.

Everything in existence has been previously dreamt by someone that held/holds the keys to creating and manifesting anything. You have the same ability, to create and manifest anything you desire, provided your frequency is at least 51% aligned with whatever it is that you desire. After the 51% there is a momentum going which you should not let slow down, otherwise you won't be able to manifest.

WHEN YOU SLEEP YOU ARE DEAD HERE BUT ALIVE ELSEWHERE. IS YOUR PHYSICAL LIFE HERE A DREAM? WHEN YOU SLEEP, IS YOUR REAL SELF ALIVE?

THE WORLD IS ANGRY, BUT WHY?

19 It seems that the world's population has been in a coma for a very long time. Countless of generations of people have come and gone without having enjoyed their lives. They have lived in poverty and suffering and for what, to just eat, drink and comply with tyranny? Throughout time, rape, violence, death, blood, anger, fear/worries are normalized and eaten (metaphorically) for breakfast, lunch and dinner. Even though I am not a religious person at all, but even the Bible says to not consume blood or else unhealed/uncleaned low frequency spirits/souls will attach to you, or another way of saying it is that those low vibration spirits will possess you. Science has already proved that. Your blood is mostly water or ultra plasma filtrate.

It has already been proven that water holds the memories of everything that passes through your blood/system. Your trillions of cells carry memories. Whether it is a human being or an animal, when the body is abused by a death lifestyle, all those memories remain in you or in the animals. In the case of the animals, the terror (low vibration frequency) that they go through, remains in their cell even after they are cooked. Consequently, it is passed onto the person that consumed the rotten body (meat). The word "meat" is a bastardization of the word "Ma'at" the Goddess of the Earth. By eating meat (or Ma'at) your heart cannot be any lighter than one of her feathers. The Goddess=ANGEL.

Isn't it interesting that angels are always depicted with feathers? Angel is an anagram for angle. The **Sun=Angles/Angels of light**. You are light condensed in flesh and bones. Your physical body is but a shell of who you truly are which is Light, consciousness/spirit. For as long as you identify yourself with your physical body and ignoring your spiritual power, you will struggle.

Many people numb themselves to death with alcohol, drugs, and all sorts of poisonous foods, drinks and digital content where they end up becoming zombies and not thinking for themselves. There are also a lot of people that make fun or look down on people that drink or have other addictions, but these very same people themselves have addictions. One simple example is "coffee". Coffee is a neurotoxin poison which the body uses a lot of its water to expel.

When you read or want to think rationally about foods or drinks, make sure that you don't think with your stomach or your taste buds. A lot of people defend coffee because coffee is a drug. Those people (including me at one point) defend it because they don't see it as a bad thing because coffee is legal. Many of those people look down on those that smoke canabis, why? Because up until a certain point canabis was illegal (and it still is in many places in the world). Those people have been conditioned to belive morality comes from the government/legality.

Humanity has suffered for as long as there has been governments or any other forms of authority. The need for authority derives from living an unconscious ignorant life. Usually, we people have grown accustomed to certain drinks, foods or other habits and when someone points at us about an unhealthy habit, we tend to defend our choices. That's an ego driven personality. An intelligent person would hear advice without having to believe it. But when we outright reject something we deny the possibility that the advice we denied could be very useful to us.

People function in anger, worries, and survival states. All these are creations of outside forces to keep us fighting each other. We are one another. The sooner we realize this, the sooner our society will become free, healthy and prosperous. Prosperity doesn't just mean money. The biggest wealth is a clear mind, under controlled emotions and a disciplined mindset. Without these we will continue to be treated as bottom feeders by those that don't have empathy toward sentient beings.

You are the wizard or the witch that they couldn't burn. There is a reason why you are alive at this time.

Do you know why?

IF YOU WANT TO STOP STRUGGLING, BECOME
YOUR OWN AUTHORITY. HELP OTHERS GET UP.
EMPOWER AND BUILD THE HEAVEN WITHIN

KUNDALINI

KUNDALINI – THE SAVIOUR OF YOUR SOUL

20 Kundalini is a snake/serpent like energy coiled at the base of the spine, or another way of describing it is like a coiled silver cord plugged into Akasha, the same cord that connects you with the ALL, the seen and the unseen - the EVERYTHING. Activation of kundalini is also known as the holy spirit or Shakti, depending on which traditions your information is fed from. When you awaken the kundalini what happens is the initiation to enlightenment by unifying the body, mind and the spirit. This results in an expanded state of consciousness. In this state you are lead to a magnificent state of being. The moment the kundalini is awaken or ignited, it will move up through the main seven energy centers or chakras, which then burns all the energy blockages.

The serpent represents rebirth and transformation. The serpent was revered in all ancient cultures. The snake is seen as an evil creature/animal in the modern world because the black magicians don't want people to look into the ancient knowledge and find out about the kundalini. The kundalini has an immense source of energy. Kundalini is dormant in most people. What keeps the Kundalini dormant?

If you keep consuming processed foods/drinks, meat , alcohol and especially sex (**porn, masturbation, ejaculation, orgasm**) that is not tantric with genuine loving intention from both partners, then you may have a violent kundalini awakening (physical, emotional and mental chaos/discomfort), but the kundalini will never rise if you do those things in bolded writing. It could only awaken violently or not, but that's it, it will not be fully raised. But if you take care of your body and your mind, especially by practicing the Super Conscious Kundalini awakening process (check the *2024 Calendar for all zodiac signs - Kundalini Awakening* chapter), then this magnificent energy (kundalini) will ascend all the way up until it reaches the top of the head and passes through the Crown chakra. When this happens, a sacred mystical experience is achieved known as Kundalini Awakening. But in fact, it is Kundalini both awakening and rising. Awakening it is not enough, just as when you open your eyes in the rising (morning) is not enough, you have to move the energy throughout your body by moving your legs, arms etc., for you to go somewhere and doing activities. When you reach this mystical awakening state of Kundalini, you will see proof of the Source of all. You will be able to tap into transcendental knowing or gnosis.

Do not drink alcohol as it suppresses the release of Vasopressin. Not only that you shouldn't drink alcohol anyway, but even if you stop drinking the day before the 3.5 days of Christ Oil practice time (the days that the Moon is in your zodiac Sun sign), you will not be able to raise the Kundalini. Alcohol stays for days in your system. So, to be safe do not drink alcohol for a whole month before the special practice days (*chapter 24*). Another thing that many do not know is that even if you don't drink alcohol you may still be an alcoholic. How? It is custom in the world that people eat cooked food accompanied by all sorts of vegetable or fruit salads. Fruit and vegetables have a much shorter digestion time than cooked foods.

Here's a general idea of the time it takes for foods to be digested, meaning when they completely leave the stomach.

> **Water** – zero digestion time
> **Juices** – 20 minutes
> **Raw Fruit** – 20-40 minutes
> **Raw Vegetables** – 30-50 minutes
> **Starchy Foods** – 1 hour
> **Grains** – 1.5 hour
> **Legumes** – 2 hours
> **Nuts and Seeds** – 2.5-3 hours
> **Meats** – 8h

So, the fruit and vegetables ferment in your stomach if you had them with cooked food which take longer to digest. Fermented food=Alcohol especially when consumed with acidic foods such as meat, processed foods/drinks etc. There is no way to greatness without great effort. You must stop consuming death if you want to become alive. Most people have no idea what being truly alive means. Being alive is not merely being able to walk, talk and breathe. These things are elementary.

> "The word "KUNDALINI" generally refers to that dimension of energy, which is yet to realize its potential. There is a huge volume of energy within you which is yet to find its potential. It is just there waiting, because what you call as a human being is still in the making. Currently you are a "JOURNEY". There is much more for you to do so that you can become the "DESTINATION". Sheer willpower, determination and discipline will make sure you arrive at the destination.

To awaken and raise your kundalini, you must save the sacred seeds which is produced once a month in your brain. This substance will travel back down the spine and rest for three and a half days in the sacrum. This represents the Christ's burial in the tomb being dormant. If this sacred seed or substance is not destroyed within the 3.5 days, then it will travel back up the spine creating a resurrection experience a.k.a. rebirth or kundalini rising. At a later chapter you'll read the days on when you have to practice the Christ consciousness or the Kundalini awakening. Your body produces **CSF**, short for CerebroSpinal Fluid.

> The cerebrospinal fluid is the highest known element that is contained in the human body. This great river of life must be tapped and with the withering field irrigated at once, or the harvest of health will be forever lost. The Cerebro Spinal Fluid is one of the rivers of life, the other two are the blood and semen. You must turn the waters of life loose at the brain (this is about the CSF), remove all hindrances and the great work (**the raising of the Kundalini or the Christ Consciousness**) will be done, and give you the eternal legacy, longevity.

In your brain, there are fluid filled ventricle cavities. At the center of your brain at the same location of your third eye (your brow center), there is a cavity called *"the third ventricle"*. The third ventricle is a midline space. It's boundaries are the Pituitary gland in the front and the Pineal gland in the back, the Thalamus and the Hypothalamus on the side. The space between these structures has been called the "Crystal Palace" and the "Cave of Brahma" in some yoga Hindu traditions. This space is filled with fluid. This fluid is called The **C**erebral **S**pinal **F**luid or **CSF** for short. This CSF is a central component of the human body. This fluid plays a crucial role in the nervous system. Our society lives an anxious life, in fear. We are living in a psychotic environment.

People's nervous systems have been damaged through all kinds of poisons such as, processed foods, processed drinks, lack of sleep, overworking for corporations, non-harmonized relationships, damaging frequencies from devices, lack of vitamin D a.k.a SUN (store bought vitamins and supplements are garbage). Your body is designed to be fed with light. What is "LIGHT"? The Sun is light. You can only put the Sun on your skin. How do you put the Sun in your belly? To eat the Sun you have to thank the plant world. The fruit, vegetables, herbs and nuts have done the work for you. All you have to do is enjoy them.

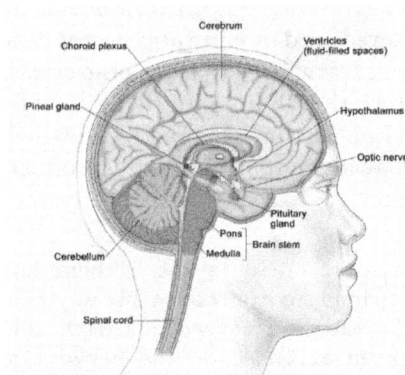

The Sun is the saviour/savior. You are your own savior by aligning with nature. When you do that, your body will function as intended. Otherwise you may only have a violent kundalini awakening but you cannot raise your kundalini if you deny what makes the kundalini rise.

Conserving (not wasting) your sexual energy (did you read about the **S**exual **E**nergy **E**xchange a few chapters earlier?) and not destroying this sacred seed or substance through sex or acidic foods/drinks will cause the Kundalini to awaken first and then be raised. To be raised is not easy if you refuse to let go of earthly attachments. Our internal organs were originally meant to elevate our consciousness, the consciousness is elevated when the energy flows freely in the body without hindrances. If you abuse your body (the shell of the real you) through foods, drinks, laziness, un-creativity etc., the energy becomes stagnant and diseases will begin to manifest.

> Your body will first whisper before screaming at you. Pay attention, your body talks to you at all times. Don't block its voice with distractions.

One major way to awaken and raise your kundalini is through breathing meditation techniques. Breathing is one of the most if not the most important aspect of human health. Most people are shallow breathers. Irregular and shallow breathers cause loss of intelligence. Getting stuck in memories of the past or imagining the future makes one to shallow breathe. Try and catch yourself when you are overthinking or when you watch a suspense movie, you'll see that you don't take deep breaths. To breathe consciously is to be in the moment.

Breath 10 times in short bursts and then take one deep breath and you'll see which one feels better. A deep breath is when all your lungs, including your diaphragm expand. Have you ever seen a depiction of Buddha with a big belly? His big belly doesn't mean that Buddha (regardless of such entity existed or not) was fat. It means that he was taking deep conscious breaths. When you take deep proper breaths, your belly swells and that's the healthiest indication that you breathe properly.

In the next chapter you'll read about a couple of breathing techniques that can help yourself in the awakening and the raising of the Kundalini. As always, there is no such thing as an easy way out. You can't just abuse your body through food, alcohol, porn etc., and expect to raise you Christ Consciousness/Kundalini by practicing breathing techniques.

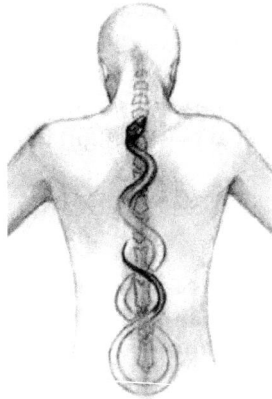

The cerebrospinal fluid is a clear colorless/colourless liquid that serves as a protective and nourishing agent for both the brain and the spinal cord residing within the brain's ventricles which can be visualized as cavities. CSF plays a vital role in cushioning these critical areas. Beside the internal aspect, this liquid also envelops the outer part of the brain's external surface providing an additional layer of protection.

The Cerebrol Spinal Fluid continues its path down the spinal cord flowing through the center canal and bathing the external surface of the spinal cord as well. The human body contains about 150ml of CSF at any given time. This fluid replenishes daily. Every day your body generates half a litre of this liquid. Amazing, isn't it?

This process is to ensure protection of your spine, brain and nervous system but also to ensure longevity and immortality. Do you realize how amazing the human body is? It is a pity to abuse it through man-made poisons. Your blood, urine, CSF and semen are the 4 rivers of life.

Just in case you are a woman reading this, you too produce an equivalent substance for semen. You must conserve it through chastity or if you do have sex it must be white tantric where neither you nor him waste the sexual substance (sacred seed).

Take care of the four rivers, if they are polluted you will not enter the Crystal Palace or the Garden of Eden. The only way to achieve this is by raising the Kundalini and achieving a Christ Consciousness state. All rivers must be clean to achieve that.

THE BLOOD, CFS (CEREBRO SPINAL FLUID),
URINE AND SEMEN ARE THE FOUR RIVERS OF
LIFE.

THIRD EYE - PINEAL GLAND

"If the doors of perception were cleansed, everything would appear to man
as it is: Infinite." – William Blake

The pineal gland or the third eye produces a masculine electrical substance known as honey which contains DMT [Dimenthyltryptamine]. This melatonin is then released in the blood and the brain [cerebrospinal fluid CSF] together with the magnetic feminine (milk) substance. The melatonin hormone regulates the body's daily (circadian rhythm) clock. Melatonin is secreted according to the amount of daylight a person is exposed to. People that are exposed less time in day light, such as the ones that work for many hours withing buildings [jobs] have trouble with their system, their mood and wellbeing. If this sacred seed or substance is not destroyed within the 3.5 days when the Moon is in your Sun/zodiac sign, it will then travel back up to the spine creating a resurrection experience, a.k.a. rebirth/kundalini rising.

This secretion/chrism oil substance goes up and down the spine once a month and remains in the tomb/dormant until it is time to wake up and travel again back up the spine and into the pineal again. The pineal gland is the center where the hypnosis is received as well as where clairvoyant visions are revealed. With a blocked pineal gland, you cannot have any visions of the future. With an opened third eye you can foretell the future.

A blocked third eye can also be a result of closed-minded ways of being/thinking. The third eye is a small pea-sized gland located behind and in alignment with the third eye chakra in the middle of the forehead, also residing in between the two hemispheres of the brain and has a pinecone shaped appearance like a raisin. The pineal gland is physical while the third eye chakra is non physical.

The name '*pineal*' literally comes from the Latin word 'pinea' which means "pinecone". The pineal gland secretes melatonin which serves in regulating sleep patterns. Melatonin protects the body from free radicals. Melatonin is also the most potent anti-cancer agent. There is no surprise as to why the governments and mega corporations promote poisons that block the pineal gland. Many fake studies have been produced to discredit the benefits of the pineal gland and many other natural cures that we now know about. Why do you think the tap water is fluoridated? They fluoridate it so the pineal gland slows down the production of melatonin. No wonder health deterioration has become the norm in our society.

With a closed pineal gland, people have trouble sleeping or they stay awake until late before they go to sleep. The pineal gland produces melatonin at night when there is total darkness. Most people are glued to their technological devices/screens until late at night. When they go to bed it is too late, the time has passed when the pineal gland works at full speed.

> "The pineal gland is not technically a part of
> the brain; it is not protected by the blood brain
> barrier. It exists in the approximate geometric
> center of the brain's mass. It has a hollow interior
> filled with a watery fluid, and receives more blood
> flow than any other part of the body except for the
> kidneys. Since it is not protected by the blood
> brain barrier, the fluid inside the pineal gland
> gathers an increasing amount of mineral deposits,
> or "brain sand" over time, which have optical and
> chemical properties similar to the enamel on your
> teeth. This calcification appears as a bonelike mass

in the center of your brain on an X ray or MRI." –
David Wilcock

Your body requires melatonin, it is an essential component of beings
that have a soul. The pineal gland or the third eye is also known as
the psychic center. Havin a blocked pineal gland is like standing in
front of a wall not knowing that outside of it there are people, forests,
seas, stars etc. The dark forces target this area of the body the most
because they know how powerful people can be when they have an
open pineal gland. Someone with an open pineal gland obeys to no
authority and fear is non-existent.

The dark forces through their devious schemes kept humanity
ignorant, uninformed and unable to think for themselves. Humans
have lost their natural born psychic abilities. Every single one has
psychic abilities, even you. The secret societies are very well aware
the implications that fluoride does to our pineal gland

HOW DO YOU OPEN YOUR PINEAL GLAND?

SUN – The third eye thrives on natural light. Both the Moon and the
Sun can have their own benefits. Take sun baths but also Moon baths.
Try to Sun/Moon bath where there are not many or no clouds at all.
Cloud may cloud your judgement. Every time you meditate or look at
the Sun or the Moon keep your focus on your third eye. Energy flows
where your attention goes.

The Light from the Sun is one of the best methods to open your pineal
gland. This must be done early in the morning or before dark. So, in
the first hour when the sun rises and the last hour before the sun sets.
Well, technically the Sun never rises, nor sets, but it's how it looks to
us. The further an object goes the smaller it becomes and it seems as
if it were going below the horizon.

CHANTING/**MUSIC** – When you meditate you can chant the syllable
OM or AUM (AAAUUUM) . Before meditating prepare you third eye
chakra mudra.

Hold your hands in the lower part of your chest, the middle fingers tips must touch and point away from you, the thumbs touch and point toward you, the other fingers bend at the first joint.

In general, music is very good to help the opening of the pineal gland, especially classical music, but the A (E) scale is associated with the third eye. There are 7 full musical notes for 7 chakras. If the music you listen to is not in A scale you can convert it to any scale you want, online or by downloading an app on your phone.

Rimias K. Neo in the book *Gain Wisdom Through Practiced Knowledge* wrote this about the music scales in relation to the chakras.

A word about the Musical Scale for each chakra.

The vibrational frequencies of the main seven chakras are supposed to correctly match their color. These new chakra vibrations is the revolutionary new European periodical system of Planetary Healing Vibrations discovered by H. Cousto in the 1970's which is based on 432hz. Many studies have shown the effectiveness of these planetary frequencies and the New Chakra Vibrations which start at the Root Chakra on G (A=432 Hz) and not with the musical note C, often used in the U.S., arbitrarily chosen from the Western diatonic music scale on C.

In parenthesis beside the musical scale, the musical scale/tone is based on the discovery of H. Cousto. Regardless of which one is the accurate, the one in parenthesis or the one without, you are the one to decide by having done more research (and personally experienced these tones) on your own. We are still in search for more pieces (of the puzzle) of truths.

Throughout this book, I have mentioned a few times tidbits from

Rimias K. Neo's book. That's because that book is still fresh in my mind. It is one of the latest books that I read and I really enjoyed it. I love the way he thinks.

DARKNESS – The pineal gland needs darkness to fully release melatonin. Just as you train your muscles when you exercise, so does the pineal gland exercise with the darkness at night or sunshine during the day. The pineal gland is very sensitive so make sure there is total darkness in the room when you sleep. If you nap during the day, try to close the curtains and help your pineal gland so it can help you. A baby grows in darkness in the womb, so does the pineal gland become alive in the dark away from the pollution.

CONSCIOUS BREATHING – Breathing consciously is a must to keep you in the present. Usually when we meditate our mind wonders in all kinds of memories and imaginations. You may forget what you are doing when meditating so make sure to consciously breathe so you can be in the moment.

AFFIRMATIONS - Affirmations are very important also. You are what you think, you say what you think and you do what you say. What you say you become. Anything you say with conviction helps you gain confidence, clarity and empowerment. When you are not scared or worried you transcend your ego to work for you. Meaning that you become resilient, you can tame your ego from being in a lazy negative mindset into an active and determined person which in turn you can manifest anything you say such as: *My pineal gland is already open*. Your brain believes anything you say to it. So, if you say that your pineal gland is already open, you are affirming therefore your brain believes it but you must repeat it daily. It takes a few days for something to become a habit. Anything you do without thinking too much is because it has become a habit.

Here are some affirmations you can practice while meditating or anytime of the day either by thinking or saying them out loud.

(a) I (say/think your NAME) am capable of perceiving energies and entities around me with my inner sight.

(b) I (say/think your NAME) can perceive auras and a person's energies via my inner sight.

(c) I (say/think your NAME) recognize clairvoyance as an ability that I

can learn.

(d) I (say/think your NAME) allow the universe to guide me in improving my clairvoyance.

Even if you think you don't have this ability yet, by affirming it, you are paving the way to opening your pineal gland and develop these abilities. Sometimes the clairvoyance ability might activate by itself. Don't panic, just ground yourself, stay centered and have no fear. I see and feel spirits around me and in the house and I am not afraid. Where you are right now, if your clairvoyant ability was developed you would see that there are spirits everywhere.

No spirit can harm you if you don't give consent. Anytime you feel that you might be in danger, just say in your mind "*I do not give consent to any spirit to contact me unless that spirit has a genuine intention to help me*". Any spirit has to obey your free will because that is a universal law. Anytime anyone obeys, does so by consent. Even if a spirit or a physical person convinces you to do something against your will (assuming no physical force happened), you are the one that consented. For example, if you took the vaccine, you walked to the place to get vaccinated. You cannot blame the government or parents or the boss at work for requiring you to be vaccinated. People or governments will take advantage of anyone that doesn't know their power.

....

Also, before I forget, try to also write with your left hand. I do not know your age and whether you know it or not, but a few decades ago, even as far back as a 100 years ago the black magicians controlling our way of life made sure that in school people wrote with their right hand as opposed to with the left. Many teachers, in certain countries would even slap the students for writing with their left hand. The left part of your body is responsible for the right part of your body and vice versa. The right side of the brain is about creativity. Those in power wanted people to become dumb and not creative. A creative person functions beyond the herd mindset reality.

Traits of someone with a blocked pineal gland
(a) A person with a blocked pineal gland has a clouded reasoning, making it difficult to arrive at a healthy conclusion or not arriving at all.

(**b**) Someone with a blocked pineal gland can have vivid dreams that are scary/nightmares or not dreaming at all. Well, everyone dreams anyway, I means that the dreams will not be remembered/recalled.

(**c**) Someone with a closed pineal gland has difficulty or inability to realistically anticipate the future, he rejects ideas that surround the spiritual and ethereal realities/realms.

(**d**) You will have difficulties putting individual thoughts and ideas into a clear, bigger picture. Picture yourself on the ground and also on the roof of a tall building. In which scenario do you see clearer?

You may want to help your pineal gland open through the use of stones/crystals. Some of these stones are: Labradorite, Fluorite (not fluoride :), Angelite, Moonstone. Practicing all these should help you restore balance to your mind, body and spirit. Do not overwhelm yourself. Do one thing at a time.

Fire is well-known that it can keep negative energies/spirits away from the area that you live. In the house, light a candle, every night if you can. Candles contain elemental spirits that burn negative energies. Candles are your friends my friend. Never put out a candle unless it's about hazards situation where the fire could burn the house. Always let the whole candle burn until there's no more candle left.

Don't just focus on your third eye. All chakras must be opened one by one. If you focus too much on one chakra, you might create blockages in the other ones. Whatever you do, be gentle, do it with genuine intention and go with the flow of your intuition and everything will be fine. With an open pineal gland, you see things as they truly are. Just as William Blake said (*read again his quote at the beginning of this subchapter*), cleanse your perception of what you think reality is. Our eyes are only so we can look at the physical world around us. You can truly see through the third eye, the all-seeing eye, the seat of the soul.

BREATHING MEDITATION TECHNIQUES FOR AWAKENING & RAISING YOUR KUNDALINI

21 Breathing is very important in awakening your kundalini and achieving Christ Consciousness or the pinacle of enlightenment as far as this realm goes. Visualization is equally important in causing the universe to arrange the circumstances required to satisfy the visualization magnetism. Everything is electromagnetism. What you think, if you think/visualize it strongly enough, it will manifest. Yes, you are that powerful. Practice these breathing methods in combination with conserving your sexual energy and taking care of your physical body, mental/emotional state and you will reach heights never thought would be possible. There is more than one way to arrive at the truth. Some techniques may be for you and some may be useful to others. Fortunately, we live in times where information is out in the open. Internet, including YouTube and many other books have so much information that you could not possible read and absorb everything in one single life time. Without further ado let's move onto the techniques.

TECHNIQUE #1 From the book *Gain Wisdom Through Practiced Knowledge* by Rimias K. Neo

....

7 minute Kundalini Awakening
INHALE for 7 seconds (inhale by using all the capacity of your lungs, including your *diaphragm) through your nose while visualizing a bright white light/energy from your crown going down the spine to the root chakra, where the serpent/kundalini is laying dormant. When you begin counting, open up your heart, your shoulders must go back, arch your spine toward you back, gently, and chin slightly

up. At the end of your 7 counts when you take all your breath in, you must engage the root triple lock steps by …holding…

HOLD your breath for 7 seconds while squeezing/contracting at the same time your:

(**a**) -pelvis floor muscles
(**b**) -perineum/anus muscles and
(**c**) -stomach muscles

While you hold your breath for 7 seconds in this triple root lock, your energy will multiply, it will stir the snake that is coiled at your root. In these 7 seconds that you are holding your breath, visualize that white light/energy that you previously brought down the spine from the crown chakra, visualize it in your root chakra as if it is getting even brighter and bigger like a giant diamond shining. After the 7 seconds of holding your breath…exhale…

EXHALE through your mouth for the duration of another 7 seconds. While you exhale through the mouth, curve your spine toward the front into a 'C' shape while you bring your arms on top of your thighs. As you do this exhale, visualize that dazzling magnificent white light traveling back up the spine and onto the crown.

All this root triple lock and the circular motion of the spine will stimulate your cerebrospinal fluid and your kundalini nerves (Ida, Pingala and Sushumna). Your spinal cord floats in that living water

(CSF). Water is life, most people use the words 'life' and 'alive' but they don't have any idea what truly being alive means.

....

TECHNIQUE #2 From the book *Natural Treasure – Quest for Knowledge, health & Freedom* by Blake Cyrier

PREPARATION

(1)<u>Empty stomach</u>: It's crucial to practice this breathing on an empty stomach, preferably upon rising (getting up in the morning) or after 3-4 hours of eating.

(2)<u>Posture</u>: Cross your legs, lean forward and place your hands above the knees, with your fingers pointing toward each other.

(3) Perform a "**lion's breath**" exhale from your mouth to eliminate the excess gases from your lungs. After this, NOSE breathing only!

Lion's breath *is a form of pranayama-a breathing exercise from the yogic tradition. This technique involves forceful exhalation through the mouth with the tongue extended and stretched down toward the chin.*

BEGIN

(**1**) Inhale Deeply: Fill your lungs with air, increasing their capacity.

(**2**) Exhale fully: Exhale all air from your lungs, while keeping your abdomen tight. This is a controlled "forced exhalation."

(**3**) Hold the Breath: After exhaling, hold the breath. Do not inhale.

(**4**) Engage the Abdominals: While holding your breath, pull your abdominal muscles inward and upward, as if trying to touch the back of the spine with your abdominal wall. This is known as bandha (Sanskrit for lock or hold). Check the image below.

(5) Hold and Release: Maintain this position for as long as it's comfortable, ideally 10-15 seconds for beginners. You'll find that your diaphragm and organs lift upward, creating a hollow cavity in the abdominal region.

(6) Inhale and Relax: Release the abdominal lock, then inhale deeply, allowing your abdomen to return to its normal position.

After a few rounds, you will feel peculiar sensations on your back ribcage. The blood is circulating intensely throughout your body. The more you do this over a period of time, the more you will revitalize its benefits. Do this before bed and you may experience wild/vivid dreams. *End of the technique #2*

I highly suggest you get both of these books, there is a lot of useful and powerful information in them. Both of these techniques will help you awaken and raise your kundalini. Of course, if you do not want to violently awaken your kundalini, you should refrain from alcohol, porn, sex, processed store-bought products etc. Kundalini is energy, and for the energy to freely awaken and rise there shouldn't be any obstacle in its path.

DEEP BREATHING MEANS EXPANSION OF LIFE, LONGEVITY.

Osho beautifully described the importance of breathing.

"Breathing has two parts. One: the body of breathing, made up of oxygen, nitrogen and so on, and two, the spirit of breathing, made up of vitality, God himself. It is just like – your body is there, and you, your consciousness, is hidden deep down in your body. The body is a protection, a vehicle. The body is the visible vehicle for the non-visible you. And the same is the case with every breath. The breath itself is just the outer layer; hidden deep in it is life itself. If you simply go on breathing and thinking that this is just air coming in and going out you will never be able to penetrate the mystery of it. And you will remain completely oblivious of yourself. Then you will remain rooted in the body. You will never be able to know that which goes beyond the body, that which is within but yet beyond, that which is hidden in the body but not obstructed by the body, not limited by the body. A beyond within. In each breath that life has to be discovered. Yoga calls those methods PRANAYAMA."

The word PRANAYAMA means expansion of life. One has to expand life to infinity in each breath. Buddha has called his own methods of discovering the innermost core of breath ANAPANA-SATI yoga: the yoga, the science, of incoming and outgoing breath; and Buddha has said no other yoga is needed. If you can watch deeply your own breathing, and watch so meditatively that anything that is hidden in the breath does not remain hidden but becomes revealed, you will come to know all. Looks simple, it is difficult but not impossible. Buddha said to his monks:

```
"Sitting, walking, standing, whatever you are doing,
go on doing these things, but let your consciousness
be aware of the breath coming in and going out.
Go on looking at your own breath, one day with the
very continuous hammering on the breath, the temple
opens."
```

What you eat is equally important. Use a dehydrator to dry bananas, apples (or others fruit) slices and seal them the same way you would/seal pickles (canning). You can use them as snacks, with zero additives. This way you defeat cravings through natural food. Most people fry things in oil. Even if you use olive oil or coconut oil which are the best, they still may oxidize when heated. So, to eliminate having to cook in oil many times, I suggest you purchase a steamer. I have been using a steamer for many years.

You can steam any vegetables with just one cup of water, no oil. When you are done steaming, then you can add fresh raw oil to consume it. And if you are still using a microwave, get rid of it as soon as possible. When you buy food products, take them off the plastic bags/container and keep them in glass containers. Glass doesn't leach any chemicals but plastic does. You may think that the product was already in the plastic bag when you bought it. My answer: You have no control over what others did, you only have control on what you do from this moment and on.

Do not waste energy on *what ifs*, **what could have happened** etc., live in the moment, make the present count toward a healthier future. What you eat is important, how you eat is important? Hmm? *"How you eat?"* You might answer: "I eat with my mouth, grab the food and put it in my mouth". By "how you eat?" I meant whether you eat fast, whether you chew the food until it becomes like a liquid in your mouth before swallowing it. Your stomach doesn't have any teeth. That's what the teeth in your mouth are for. Follow this rule,

"Eat the liquids and drink the solids". This means that any liquid is to be drank very slow, and also in portions. And the solid food is to be chewed until it becomes a liquid, hence *"eat the liquids and drink the solids"* phrase.

Also, never drink while you eat. When you eat, your mouth and your stomach produce digestive enzymes to ease the work of your system. If you drink you wash down those enzymes. Make it a habit to not drink until one hour before eating and one hour after eating, Unless you're choking on food which in that case you have to drink water.

SHORT AND IRREGULAR BREATHS MEANS
"D.E.A.T.H". DEEP BREATHS MEANS
"L.I.F.E"

KUNDALINI AWAKENING SYMPTOMS

22 Depending on how cleansed your body is, you might have an amazing and beautiful kundalini awakening or you might have a violent one. As an example, if you are an alcoholic, or if you drink alcohol in general you must not attempt to awaken the kundalini.

What are some of the symptoms of the kundalini awakening?

(**1**)*You feel like you are one with the source, the creation/creator of all.*

(**2**)*You feel more creative, your pineal gland is glowing and* causing you to expand your creativity.

(**3**)You become more empathetic toward animals and humans or any sentient beings.

(**4**)*You are not getting bothered anymore with past trauma. You are not enslaved anymore by memories of the past problems/mistakes and/or the imagining of the supposed future as a result of living in a fear/worry/survival mode.*

(**5**)*You become an observant person. You are not diving anymore in the middle of the battlefield (arguing or fighting with people). You understand that anything that anyone says is simply an expression from the reality that they live (which they created) in the moment.*

(**6**)*Your energy is raised tenfold. Boredom is a thing of the past, you feel like you always have to do something, you are full of energy.*

(**7**)*You have trouble sleeping because the energy of the awakened kundalini is very powerful. In this case the discomfort is because your kundalini was not awakened incrementally but something forced it such as, alcohol or a traumatic experience etc.*

Kundalini awakening and Kundalini rising is not the same thing. If you want to get from point A to Point B you will not get there by just turning on your car and stay on the same spot. You have to drive to get there. The same applies here, where kundalini awakening is but the first step in directing that energy all the way up through the spine and onto the pineal gland, crown chakra and beyond.

Kundalini energy is seen as demonic by many religious people. Jinn or Djinn in Islam is a supernatural spirit state which you can achieve. Achieving Christ Consciousness or Jinn state is the same thing. A *fake Christian or a *fake Muslim would think/see Christ Consciousness spirits or Jinns as demons because religions don't want people to achieve these states. In these states you have absolutely no need by anyone externally to guide you. This is a state of Bliss when you achieve it. When people achieve these higher states of mind, then religions have zero power, they cannot control people anymore.

By fake Christians or fake Muslims or any other fake religious people I mean that they have had the truth all along in those religious books but they listen to the Church/Mosques and read those books literally. Their hearts are in the right place, but not their mind. Being a *"good human being"* must also be accompanied with a mind that can think for itself or else it can be hijacked as it has already been by religions, more accurately hijacked by those that have used religions as a **WMD** [*weapon of mass destruction/distractions*] or **WOC** [*weapon of control*].

```
Some times the Kundalini will spontaneously
awaken by itself. When you force its awakening,
it may be a violent one.
```

So, it's best to eat healthy, conserve your sexual energy, exercise, practice breathing techniques, practice solitude etc. without having to worry about the Kundalini. Even if you didn't know anything about the Kundalini energy, you have to take care of your body, mind and soul anyway.

YOU POSSESS THE GREATEST GIFT
EVER GIVEN TO A SENTIENT BEING

KUNDALINI BOOSTER DRINKS

23 Here's a couple of boosters that can help in the activation of the Kundalini. As with any information, nothing is just a black and white statement. Sometimes, even though some information could make 100% sense, it doesn't mean that it will be accurate for everyone. Something works better for some people than for others. You can't drink alcohol daily and by consuming these juices you'd think you would awaken the kundalini. If you do awaken it, in this case it would be a violent awakening. Violence doesn't just mean physically. Violence can be mental or emotional also.

If you are an alcoholic, you could even die if your kundalini awakening is very violent. Kundalini is not a joke, you must already be on the path to mental, emotional and spiritual health before attempting to awaken it. If you drive a brand-new car with dirty oil/gas, how long do you think it would last? It will break fast. So, make sure you fast regularly, exercise, practice deep breathing techniques etc. if you want a soft, and pleasurable kundalini awakening.

The Kundalini will awaken by itself without any discomfort if you pay attention to what you eat, drink, think, say and do. When do you feel better? When you wake up from an alarm clock to be forced to work for a corporation or when you naturally wake up on your day off without any alarms or external noises? You already know the answer.

Here are a couple of recipes form the book
Natural Treasure by Blake Cyrier

FIRE in the hole
*1 lemon, 8 carrots, 8 dandelion leaves, 2 green apples. 1 inch ginger root, 2 stalks celery, ¼ **jalapeno**, 1 beet. Add ingredients to a masticating juicer. Pour juice into 32oz jar and enjoy.*

Breath FIRE
I bunch kale, 1 bunch celery, 1 bunch dill, 1 cucumber, 1 green apple, 1

habanero pepper. *Add ingredients to a masticating juicer, pour juice into 32oz jar. Cheers!*

Guns, bombs & green-aides
*1 lemon, 1 inch ginger root, 1 green apple, 1 cucumber, 1 bunch celery, 1 bunch parsley, ½ **jalapeno**, waters of 1 coconut (1-2 cups). Add ingredients to a masticating juicer. Pour juice into 32oz jar. Bottoms up.*

All of the recipes in his books are healthy but I specifically/on purpose chose these three where pepper is one of the ingredients. Hot pepper opens up your blood vessels. When the blood vessels are opened up, the blood freely flows. When the blood is free and clean, you cannot age and you will not die. For this to happen you must give up on anything that you previously thought was healthy. There is no way to health without hopping over some obstacles. If you have any severe conditions, do your own research before consuming hot pepper. The greatest rule to follow for when there is something wrong with your health is to fast. If you don't feel good, fast. If you have a headache, fast. Do a short fast as a start until you get used to fasting for longer periods of time.

Even though Blake Cyrier doesn't speak much about the Kundalini in his book, everything written in his book contributes to the awakening and the raising of the kundalini. The kundalini will fully awaken when your internal energy is clear and free flowing. How does it flow freely? By what you drink, eat, how much you eat, if you fast or not, if you exercise or not, if you sleep enough and if you awaken in the rising (not morning) without the alarm or any other noise, if you practice breathing meditation, if you conserve your sexual energy etc. Blake talks about all these subjects (and much more) in his book National Treasure, except for the subject on conserving sexual energy.

On sexual energy (and many other subjects) check these books.

(1) *Body Mind Soul* by Saimir Kercanaj
(2) *Gain Wisdom Through Practiced Knowledge* by Rimias K. Neo
(3) *Man's higher consciousness* by Hilton Hotema

Nitric Oxide Kundalini booster by Kelly-Marie Kerr
You will find her on YouTube or check the YouTube link at the end of this book under Resources. In her video she explains the importance of Nitric Oxide and how it is relate to the Kundalini.

5 *cooked beetroots, 2 large carrots, 5 oranges (peeled) 1 large ginger root.

Chop all these ingredients and blend them in a blender. Enjoy.

This is a big batch. If you are just one person, then cut the recipe in half or even further. A lot of people prepare juices or smoothies for the next day. I wouldn't suggest that, for the simple fact that after half an hour or so, when the juice comes in contact with oxygen it will start to oxidize. So, make juice only when you want to consume it within half an hour of preparing/juicing.

*Personally, I use raw beets when I make home made juice or smoothies. Perhaps when you cook the beets there is a chemical reaction. Nowhere in the video does she mention the reason as for why the beets have to be cooked. It needs more research as to why this is good for the awakening of the Kundalini. But as far as health goes, you don't need to research if beets or any other fruit or vegetables are good for you.

Anything that grows from the ground (through a photosynthesis process) is good for you. Some people have discomfort when they consume certain fruit or vegetables. It is not the fruit or vegetable's fault/problem. The problem is the person who cannot tolerate certain natural foods. When you put new oil in your car's engine you would first empty the old/bad oil first wouldn't you? Every time that you are hungry, it doesn't mean that you have to eat. Your hunger hormone releases a signal to make you feel hungry. It just reminds you to eat, it is by design but you don't have to eat. Your own free will decides what you do with your own body.

THINK FOR YOURSELF AND FEEL. AND
YOU WILL REALIZE WHAT IS TRULY REAL

2025 CALENDAR FOR ALL 12 ZODIAC SIGNS – KUNDALINI AWAKENING

24 These are the days for each sun sign when you have to practice your superconscious/kundalini awakening, or the chrism oil (Christ Consciousness). At an earlier chapter I mentioned that the sacred secretion/chrism oil or substance rests dormant for 3.5 days and awaits to be raised but in this chapter/calendar you will see that I mentioned 4 and 5 days of practice. That's because it is better to begin the practice at least 12h before the date that the Moon enters your Sun/zodiac sing and to finish the practice at least 12h after the Moon exists your Sun sign. Let's say that you are ARIES, check the month (let us assume that now we are in February 2025). You will have to practice the super consciousness/kundalini awakening on February 2nd, 3rd, 4th, and 5th. And if it is later than the 5th of February, then be patient until March to practice again the same practice: no food, no conventional sex, no orgasms, no alcohol no gossiping, no lying etc. on the days under March. You should not lie, gossip etc. anyway, regardless of what the date or hour/minute of the day it is. You can eat the first and the last days but try not to eat in-between days.

By 'eating' I mean consuming only fruit, salads, vegetables. No cooked food and no solid man-made food you get from the store. The cooked food, even if it is vegetables it will lose many of its nutrients through the cooking process. If you are strong to not eat at all for 4 or 5 days, then more power to you. If you've never tried long fasts before, then eat all the days under your Sun, but light eating, until you are ready to not eat for 3 or more days another month, whenever the Moon is in your Sun sign again.

> You have the same opportunity once (or twice
> sometimes) a month to reGENErate and stop getting
> old, so pretty much you are designed to not age.

You must fast and no processed or cooked food one day before and one day after these dates, and *no sex, no orgasms, no arousal* for the whole duration of these days. You may have a Kundalini Awakening even if you infringe one of the above-mentioned ideal rules, but it doesn't mean that it will be raised all the way up to the crown chakra.

To fast for 3, 4 or 5 days on just water is very difficult for most people so try one or two days as a start, and the next month when the Moon is in your Sun sign, increase the days. You can also just juice fast in those days. Next time try just water. You are the one to decide how hard you go on your journey. Take your time, better to learn how to walk before running so you don't fall.

No sex, no orgasms, no arousal, no ejaculation (for men) – These apply only when you want to awaken the kundalini. To raise the kundalini, conserving the sexual energy (*no sex, no orgasms, no arousal*) must be a daily life routine. You can't just waste your sexual energy regularly and stop only on the days when the Moon is in your zodiac/ Sun sign. As an example, it takes 70-74 days from germ to mature sperm cell. Your sexual energy tank is full if you haven't had sex (or masturbation, arousal in general) for at least 74 days. But even then, if you had alcohol or other processed foods and/or drinks within those 74 days, your blood will still be polluted.

The point is that you have to truly put a great effort in cleansing yourself if you want your Kundalini to fully rise and achieve Christ Consciousness. Right now, I am fasting, I'm at the 40h mark. The Sun is in my zodiac Sun sign/Sagittarius. The fridge is full, I went outside for a walk in the neighbourhood and I kept smelling all kinds of flavory, beautiful foods neighbours were cooking. But I didn't give up. I decided to fast for at least 72h. Why 72hours? Because that time is when the "autophagy" reaches it's maximum work/process. Autophagy means self-devouring. Which means that the body is cleaning itself, by destroying old and cancerous cells and many other foreign organisms.

For the body to do this, the digestive system has to completely stop, and for that to happen you must fast on just water for at least 36hours, that's when autophagy ramps up. I am not going to talk about fasting here but check on Amazon for these books (which I have read) which talk about fasting:

Rational Fasting by Arnold Ehret
Body Mind Soul by Saimir Kercanaj
Fasting for Health by Anne Marie Houston

Some months have two different sets of dates where the second set of dates has half of the dates (last 2 days of the month), where the other half continues onto the next month. For example, if you are Aries you will practice the Kundalini awakening on March 1, 2, 3, 4, but also on March 29, 30, 31 and continuing practicing also on April 1 first. You have many chances in one year. Awakening it without knowing what you're actually doing or without a trained professional, there could be a violent kundalini awakening. So, don't be addicted in awakening it. It is better to practice chastity, consume natural food, meditate etc., and the Kundalini will eventually awaken and rise by itself.

---

*The **Tropical** zodiac is the position of the Sun referenced against Earth's horizon.*
*The **Sidereal** zodiac is the position of the Sun referenced against the stars.*

Bolded numbers are the tropical dates. Non-bolded numbers are the sidereal dates.

ARIES 2025

January-**6, 7**, 8, 9
February-**2, 3**, 4, 5
March-**1, 2**, 3, 4
March-**29, 30**, 31 April 1
April-**25, 26**, 27, 28
May-**23, 24**, 25, 26
June-**19, 20**, 21, 22
July-**16, 17**, 18, 19
August-**12, 13**, 14, 15
September-**9, 10**, 11, 12
October-**6, 7**, 8, 9
November-**3, 4**, 5, 6
November-**30**, December **1**, 2, 3
December-**27, 28**, 29, 30

TAURUS 2025

Bolded numbers are the tropical dates. Non-bolded numbers are the sidereal dates.

January-**8, 9**, 10, 11

February-**4, 5**, 6, 7
March-**3, 4**, 5, 6,   **31**
April-**1**, 2, 3
April-**27, 28**, 29, 30
May-**25, 26**, 27, 28
June-**21, 22**, 23, 24
July-**18, 19**, 20, 21
August-**15, 16**, 17, 18
September-**11, 12**, 13, 14
October-**8, 9**, 10, 11
November-**5, 6**, 7, 8
December-**2, 3**, 4, 5
December-**29, 30**, 31, January 1, 2026

GEMINI 2025

Bolded numbers are the tropical dates. Non-bolded numbers are the sidereal dates.

January-**10, 11**, 12, 13
February-**5, 6, 7**, 8, 9,
March-**6, 7, 8**, 9, 10
April-**2, 3**, 4, 5   **29, 30**, May 1, 2
May-**27, 28**, 29, 30
June-**23, 24**, 25, 26
July-**20, 21**, 22, 23
August-**17, 18**, 19, 20
September-**13, 14**, 15, 16
October-**10, 11**, 12, 13
November-**7, 8**, 9, 10
December-**4, 5**, 6, 7

CANCER 2025

Bolded numbers are the tropical dates. Non-bolded numbers are the sidereal dates.

January-**12, 13**, 14, 15
February-**8, 9**, 10, 11
March-**8, 9**, 10, 11
April-**4, 5**, 6, 7
May-**1, 2**, 3, 4
May-**29, 30**, 31, June 1
June-**25, 26**, 27, 28

July-**23, 24**, 25, 26
August-**19, 20**, 21, 22
September-**15, 16**, 17, 18
October-**12, 13**, 14, 15
November-**9, 10**, 11, 12
December-**6, 7, 8**, 9, 10

LEO 2025

Bolded numbers are the tropical dates. Non-bolded numbers are the sidereal dates.

January-**14, 15**, 16, 17
February-**11, 12**, 13, 14
March-**10, 11**, 12, 13
April-**6, 7**, 8, 9
May-**3, 4**, 5, 6,   **31**
June-**1**, 2, 3
June-**27, 28**, 29, 30
July-**25, 26**, 27, 28
August-**21, 22**, 23, 24
September-**17, 18**, 19, 20
October-**14, 15, 16**, 17, 18
November-**11, 12**, 13, 14
December-**8, 9**, 10, 11

VIRGO 2025

Bolded numbers are the tropical dates. Non-bolded numbers are the sidereal dates.

January-**17, 18**, 19, 20
February-**13, 14**, 15, 16
March-**12, 13**, 14, 15
April-**9, 10**, 11, 12
May-**6, 7**, 8, 9
June-**2, 3**, 4, 5,   **29, 30**, July 1, 2
July-**27, 28**, 29, 30
August-**23, 24**, 25, 26
September-**20, 21**, 22, 23
October-**17, 18**, 19, 20
November-**13, 14**, 15, 16
December-**10, 11**, 12, 13

LIBRA 2025

Bolded numbers are the tropical dates. Non-bolded numbers are the sidereal dates.

January-**19, 20**, 21, 22
February-**15, 16**, 17, 18
March-**15, 16**, 17, 18, 19
April-**11, 12**, 13, 14
May-**8, 9**, 10, 11
June-**5, 6**, 7, 8
July-**2, 3**, 4, 5 **29, 30**, 31, August 1
August-**26, 27**, 28, 29
September-**22, 23**, 24, 25
October-**19, 20**, 21, 22
November-**15, 16**, 17, 18
December-**13, 14**, 15, 16

SCORPIO 2025

Bolded numbers are the tropical dates. Non-bolded numbers are the sidereal dates.

January-**22, 23**, 24, 25
February-**18, 19**, 20, 21
March-**17, 18**, 19, 20
April-**14, 15**, 16, 17
May-**11, 12**, 13, 14
June-**7, 8**, 9, 10
July-**4, 5**, 6, 7
August-**1, 2**, 3, 4 **28, 29**, 30, 31
September-**24, 25**, 26, 27
October-**22, 23**, 24, 25
November-**18, 19**, 20, 21
December-**15, 16**, 17, 18

SAGITTARIUS 2025

Bolded numbers are the tropical dates. Non-bolded numbers are the sidereal dates.

January-**24, 25**, 26, 27
February-**21, 22**, 23, 24, 25
March-**20, 21**, 22, 23
April-**16, 17**, 18, 19

May-**13, 14**, 15, 16
June-**10, 11**, 12, 13
July-**7, 8**, 9, 10
August-**3, 4**, 5, 6   **31**, September **1**, 2, 3
September-**27, 28**, 29, 30
October-**24, 25**, 26, 27
November-**20, 21**, 22, 23
December-**18, 19**, 20, 21

CAPRICORN 2025

Bolded numbers are the tropical dates. Non-bolded numbers are the sidereal dates.

January-**27, 28**, 29, 30
February-**23, 24**, 25, 26
March-**22, 23**, 24, 25
April-**19, 20**, 21, 22
May-**16, 17**, 18, 19
June-**12, 13**, 14, 15
July-**9, 10**, 11, 12
August-**6, 7**, 8, 9
September-**2, 3**, 4, 5   **29, 30**, October 1, 2
October-**27, 28**, 29, 30
November-**23, 24**, 25, 26
December-**20, 21**, 22, 23

AQUARIUS 2025

Bolded numbers are the tropical dates. Non-bolded numbers are the sidereal dates.

January-**1, 2**, 3, 4   **29, 30**, 31, February 1
February-**24, 25, 26**, 27, 28
March-**25, 26**, 27, 28
April-**21, 22**, 23, 24
May-**18, 19**, 20, 21
June-**14, 15**, 16, 17
July-**12, 13**, 14, 15
August-**8, 9**, 10, 11
September-**4, 5**, 6, 7, 8
October-**2, 3**, 4, 5   **29, 30**, November 1, 2
November-**25, 26**, 27, 28
December-**23, 24**, 25, 26

PISCES 2025

Bolded numbers are the tropical dates. Non-bolded numbers are the sidereal dates.

January-**4, 5**, 6, 7   **31**, February **1**, 2, 3
February-**27, 28** March 1, 2
March-**27, 28**, 29, 30
April-**23, 24**, 25, 26
May-**21, 22**, 23, 24
June-**17, 18**, 19, 20
July-**14, 15**, 16, 17
August-**10, 11**, 12, 13
September-**7, 8**, 9, 10
October-**4, 5**, 6, 7   **31**, November **1**, 2, 3
November-**28, 29**, 30   December 1
December-**25, 26**, 27, 28

Do not engage in chaos, do not gossip, do not entertain negative energies. Learn to set boundaries with people. Do not surround yourself with people that don't encourage you to grow. Let your action create peace and harmony. Chaos can also bring peace but only when you recognize situations for what they are, you learn from them and move on to situations that push you higher. Especially in these days when you have to practice the kundalini awakening, be as peaceful as possible, fast as much as you can, eat (if you have to) as healthy as possible. One simple burst of anger can immediately lower your frequency.

> YOU HAVE ABOUT 12 CHANCES IN ONE YEAR. YOU CAN DO IT AND YOU KNOW IT

YOU ARE MISSING ONE MONTH
EVERY YEAR OF YOUR LIFE

25 Your physical body is designed to live continuously, and not age. If you think that aging is normal, then the conditioning has proved to be a success. It is not your fault, you were conditioned by your parents, they were conditioned by their own parent and so on, but it was unintentional from your parents part, through ignorance but unintentional nonetheless. You are an eternal everlasting spirit. You are temporary here to learn as much as you can through experiencing this world with everything it has to offer. Earth was meant to be a school and not a prison. A small group of beings/people hijacked this schooling ground (Earth) and turned it into a prison. People became prisoners.

The thugs (the group of beings who wanted us to be slaves) turned people against each other by poisoning their minds, by leading them astray, away from the natural flow of how the universe and anything natural functions. The 6th month missing is called Sextus (or Undecimber) from another period of time/calendar). Since throughout time people have added and subtracted days from different calendar systems, it is not impossible that April 1st being March 21st (when the Sun enters Aries matters and not the man-made date). Whenever April 1st was (assuming it was) the beginning of the year in the Roman times, that day could have been the day that the Sun entered Aries. Now in the current times, March 21st is the day when the Sun enters Aries. Only the dates and names change. When the Sun enters Aries doesn't change.

According to the universal clock/time (not the man made one) the celestial bodies function perfectly. Humans have assigned different names and dates according to their needs at the time. But there are needs to improve people's life and there are also needs to control people, in the case of those that made changes to put humans in a disharmonious state with nature. In the future, let's say 300 years from now, if the calendar's 1st day of the year will be on the 10th of August (assuming the calendar will be changed to keep humans enslaved) all the people at that period of time have to do is to easily find out when the Sun enters Aries and they will know when the beginning of the year will be. But to know this, is not enough, one has to also live life by using a 13-month calendar where each month has 28 days.

```
One month each year has not been counted, meaning it
has been taken out of your life. Your body has been
thinking to be one month older each year. This means
that you are younger than you actually are. Subtract
28 days for each year that you have lived so far
and you'll know your real age in this incarnation.
So, if you are 40, subtract 1,120 days or 40 months
(every month should have 28 days). Celebrating your
birthday makes it even worse. Every time you blow
out the candles you are blowing years out of your
life.
```

You may think 40 months is not a lot but if you knew that you would die tomorrow, would you want to live one more day? What about 1,120 more days?

Psychologically when you think about the number of your age, subconsciously you also know (you have been conditioned to) there is an end to your life. This means that you are casting dark spells on yourself. This dark spell is thought to have been created by the fallen angels for the purpose to keep humans age at a manageable rate, meaning manageable so that humans don't rebel against their masters. You either are a slave or a master (master of your own life in this case), you cannot be both, that would be an oxymoron.

Each one of your body's trillion of cells has its own intelligence. Each of those cells have a central switch that controls how they behave. That switch is your mind. Whatever/whoever you believe to be, the cells will obey you. So, if you think you are getting older, then the cells are designed to obey the leader which is you. Without you realizing it, you are the cause of your aging, getting sick etc.

In another calendar in a book called *GAIN WISDOM THROUGH PRACTICED KNOWLEDGE* by Rimias K. NEO, the author wrote these 13 months: March, April, May, June, July, August, September, October, November, December, **UNDECIMBER**, January and February as the last month of the year with March being the 1st month of the year since on March 21st that's when the Sun enter Aries. That would be Spring Solstice and that would be correct for March being the first month of the year. Whichever calendar is right, we are still on the right track by having re-discovered that the New Year begins in March (or April 1st) when life begins to grow, when flowers bloom, when buds from trees begin to swell.

> It is ok to research and mention dates or names as a point of reference but know that time is not accurate. Being in the moment always is.

The Gregorian calendar that the world has been using for centuries is unnatural and in disharmony with the natural rhythm of the universe. In another calendar, I have seen the missing month called SOL, which means SUN (SOLar system). See, the different names of the months that different system or civilizations used, does not matter at all. What matters is that they all had one thing in common, that each system had 13 Lunar months which meant that the **system** the people in those times lived in, **was** in harmony with the plants, the people and everything else natural.

13 moons & 28 days on all turtle shells. This equals 364 days, plus one day of rest. All indigenous people around the world knew the wisdom of the turtle and followed a 13 month calendar; after all, there are 13 moon cycles in a year & 27-29 days per cycle.

It's almost as if white man subtracted one month in order sever the connection between the people and the sun, moon & stars, which are themselves a giant clock.

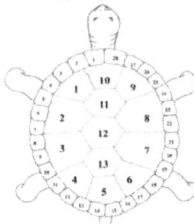

Nature (or the Creator) even printed the 13-month calendar on the back of the turtle. Aboriginals and many ancient civilizations used the back of the turtle's shell as a lunar calendar. The turtle's shell has the same pattern as the lunar months and days which would be 28 days for each month, 28 little sections all around the turtle's shell and

13 lunar months with 13 sections on the inner area of the turtle's shell. I firmly believe that if women began to practice living their life according to the 13 lunar month calendar, eventually they would stop menstruating.

There are a lot of theories as to what went on in the past, we do not really know with accuracy but one thing is true that our bodies are not in tune with the natural flow of nature. Clocks (especially when you wake up from an alarm clock) and written calendars, especially the altered ones have played a huge role in the destruction of our body's natural flow. Blood is the river of life, it should not be wasted, it must stay inside. The same applies for semen.

TIME IS NOT ACCURATE. BUT BEING
IN THE MOMENT. ALWAYS IS.

.....AND MORE

YOU ARE NEVER ALONE – SOLITUDE IS YOUR BEST FRIEND

26 Generally, people like to socialize. We are not meant to be alone. Loneliness (intentional) or solitude are simply solutions to get away from the man-made chaos. Humans are not designed to live in the mind. The mind is needed to rationalize and make wise choices to improve one's life but not to the point that it becomes detrimental to one's life. Socializing happens for two major reasons:

1- **Human nature** - to be united with other parts of yourself. Everyone else is another aspect of you.

2- **Scared of loneliness**. Loneliness and solitude are not the same thing. Loneliness happens when you do not know yourself, when you are trying to run from yourself, from worries and fears. In the long run you end up with more worries and fears. You hang around with others so that you can forget your problems or to share your problems with others because you are not strong enough to face them yourself. You end up bleeding onto others with your problems. It takes an enormous amount of energy to choose to be alone.

Most people would rather choose to be poorly surrounded by people that have their own problems to deal with. Always go for quality rather than quantity. You must build quality by working hard on yourself by chiselling away heavy parts that hold you back. You hold yourself back. The greatest connection is that with yourself. Honour yourself by finding strength in solitude.

> Solitude is an ocean that you can freely swim within the depth of the universe within. Loneliness is the pond where only your feet can get wet with what's

possible if you were to discover the ocean within.

In solitude you enjoy your life, you give others space to themselves, you don't choke them with your drama/gossiping/complaints. If you don't learn to enjoy solitude you will become co-dependent. You bind yourself to other people's needs.

They will use you and you will use them, not necessarily with bad intentions. Self-love is realized in solitude. Circumstances can only tell you what to think on what self-love is. The word SELF should tell you who must decide what something truly is. In solitude you realize who your best friend is, which means it is YOU. You can only know yourself when you enjoy your own company.

Enjoying solitude is the first step to be able to discern external people where you know with certainty who is or who is not so good for your mental and emotional self. In solitude you learn what freedom really is because you allow others to be free. Only ego wants to possess, the soul knows it's eternal. Give others freedom so that they will realize the beauty of being free.

Being in the present paints a beautiful picture of the cosmos as an ever-present web of energy and awareness. Here, we are led to realize that loneliness is a paradox because, at our core, we are never truly alone, even though it is a separate emotion. For instance, according to the notion of morphic resonance put forth by British biologist Rupert Sheldrake, we may sense the presence of ancestors or historical personalities who trod similar paths, even when we are alone. According to his theory, everyone's ideas and experiences are accessible to everyone else because we are all a part of the collective memory of our species.

Fundamentally, our metaphysical existence is at odds with the physical and emotional difficulties of loneliness. The idea of Brahman, the supreme reality that is independent of all human beings, is central to Hinduism. As components of a larger whole, we are all interdependent under Brahman. This is why the line 'The teachings of Vedanta Philosophy', which have long explored the concept of non-duality, seem to echo the idea that you are a part of something grand and eternal. This work alludes subtly to the spiritual principle of Oneness.

Eckhart Tolle's teachings on experiencing and being fully present in the here and now also reflect the spiritual aspect. A great book of Tolle's that I've read is titled THE POWER OF NOW. Mysticism about the past and future fades and a sense of oneness with the cosmic energy field is established when we let go of the concept of time and focus mostly on the here and now. I wrote mostly because sometimes you can recall beautiful moments of the past but also ugly moments of the past for the purpose of seeing those ugly moments as lessons. It is very important that when you recall those ugly moments do not engage your emotions, otherwise it is like living those feelings/emotions all over again.

From your physical point of view, the inside of your body is full of darkness since the only light source is the sun or the lights in the room. And yet, your internal body is full of light. Light is intelligence. All your cells and organs work in harmony without you doing anything. When you have a bright idea where does it come from? It comes from your mind, which is an extention of the Great MIND. There is light outside of you but also inside of you. Unless you face your own darkness (created by the fake character/ego you may think you are) your inner light will always be dim.

SOLITUDE IS FULL OF FRIENDS. DARKNESS IS FULL OF LIGHT IF YOU LEARN HOW TO SEE.

8 BILLION NONSENSE

27 Millions of people live in apartments, as do I. Cities are concrete jungles. They rob the life out of you. Next year I will move and live in the country. I don't care, as long as I have a piece of land to grow fruit and vegetables. There is enough land in the whole known, official Earth for everyone to have a small or a big piece of land. You (assuming you are living in the city and don't have any other choice) might say that it is impossible to live outside of the city. I say it is possible. That mindset is what keeps you trapped. You've heard of the phrase "demand and supply". Well, the system is supplying you with what you are demanding. Don't tell me that you had no choice. You are where you are because of you. Just as I am.

But there comes a time where you must see the bigger picture. You will not see the big picture if you keep blaming the government or any other person or the circumstances. Circumstances are created by you. You receive what you demand. If you receive what you do not want, then that is because you do not know how the law of manifestation works. You are an electromagnetic being, every thought/emotion you have, you are sending the signal out there which then you will be answered with the same signal or frequency. You might say that you have a good heart, you never hurt anyone, then how come you are still struggling?

Previously I mentioned that you are an electro-magnetic being, Which means your heart and your mind are equally important for what you attract. Having a good heart is not enough, your mind must also be in the right place or frequency. Whatever it is that you think daily, is it you that thinks those thoughts or are you replaying corrupted scenarios/made up stories (ideas or opinions) that others have injected in your mind knowingly/intentionally or unknowingly?

You've heard the word '*solitude*'. It is the only way to hear yourself, otherwise you are just going to repeat what others have told you. Or anything you read or see or hear anywhere else. When you live in a worry, fear mindset, you live in survival mode. Not only that you work for many hours in a four walled building but you do (live) the same when you go home, since you are detached from nature. You belong in nature. We are nature. Even if it may seem that your circumstances do not allow for you to live outside the city, at least think as if you are going to.

By thinking this way, you are going to attract circumstances that will satisfy your desires/demands. The universe is your servant or your master. You are the one that decides how your life flows. We cannot possibly be 8 billion of people on this Earth. Those that don't have your best interest in mind have overloaded your life with external nonsense, be it physical/materialistic or mental/emotional pollution. All the cures for your body and mind are within yourself. In life you do not possess anything. You were born with everything you'll ever need. Training and disciplining yourself is a must in life. Eva Wong in the book *Cultivating Stillness* wrote:

> You must be steadfast like stone and iron, and you must not waiver. Do not crave riches. Do not crave sexual pleasure. Do not be daunted by threats and fear. Your will must be centered, or you will abandon the path along the way. You must isolate your body from fame, fortune, possessive love, liquor, sexual pleasure, and emotions. You must cut them off with a sharp knife. You must cultivate yourself from within.

The path to true enlightenment is not easy, but it is doable when you become a determined person and develop a Godlike/Goddess like discipline. The disciplined people don't have more abilities than you or me. What they have is sheer will power and determination. When you have both will power and determination you are guaranteed to develop discipline. It doesn't matter whether there are 2, 8, 10 or 50 billion people on Earth. The only person that exists in your mind is YOU. The rest of the people are just imaginations/projections. Yes, sure you can see, hear and touch people but you are not your body. You have a physical body but even that is a projection from the Source, the GREAT MIND, the place where you are really from.

> Every one in the world that you met or that you will ever meet is your own imagination. You are the only person that exists. Take some time to think about this. You created this world and everything in it.

Please, don't get confused with who or what created everything as in "God". I am talking about your own personal reality. Imagine if you got up form a night's sleep and there were no people, no roads, no plants, no houses, nothing, you would disintegrate, you would not be able to exists for one single second in a physical body. Imagination breeds creation. People that you have never seen before do not exist. They only exist in someone else's imagination/creation. This may be a difficult concept or reality for you to grasp but ALL is MIND.

EVERY ONE YOU'VE EVER MET AND WILL EVER MEET, IS YOUR OWN CREATION. THEY ONLY EXIST IN YOUR OWN WORLD

TOMORROW NEVER ARRIVES, TOMORROW IS THE NEXT TODAY

28 Why do people worry too much about tomorrow? Why be in a rush to be in the tomorrow? What is so special about it? Either you live a mindful present or an empty one. You must live a mindful present and not a mind**FULL** one. It is one thing to be prepared for tomorrow and another to be worried and live in fearful moments of things that might happen. *"Will happen"* and *"might happen"* are two different things. One is certainty, the other is an illusion, it is a fictional possibility.

Read this story below about preventing yourself from being imprisoned by worries, fears and uncertainties.

In a small village situated between two beautiful mountains there lived a young boy named "Leo". Leo was a very generous, good hearted but God-fearing man. He used to spend most of his time in the devotion of God. He would go to Church every morning. However, he remained worried most of the day. People of the Village would say about Leo that the second name of worries in their village is Leo. He does nothing but worry. The more time passed the deeper Leo's worries grew into his character.

Leo began to spend his time thinking about unnecessary negative things like: What would he do if his mother died, or what would happen to her and the house if something happened to him? Who would take care of him if he ended up in a hospital or in a wheelchair? All these questions filled up his mind with all sorts of worries. These are foolish worries. All this foolishness caused him to be unhappy for the most part of his daily life. He was cursing God for his unhappiness. The villagers would avoid Leo whenever he would be in their way.

Due to Leo's unnecessary worries, people refused to hang around and talk to him. To pass his time, Leo would go to a beautiful river away from the village. He would sit there, in solitude under a large, beautiful tree. He thought that too much thinking and worrying had almost ruined his life. He thought that if he had to save his life and future, he would have to give up this life destroying habit (meaning WORRYING) very soon, otherwise it would take him to the boundless depth of unending depression, hopelessness and disappointment. One of the very few friends that Leo had, saw Leo sitting there.

He approached Leo and asked him: 'What happened my friend, and why are you sitting here alone?" Leo told his friend about his habit of too much worrying and overthinking. Leo's friend advised him to meet a Zen monk residing in a nearby monastery of their village. He then continued to say that the Zen master was very thoughtful and meditative and he had resolved the suffering and problems of thousands of people. If you go there you will also have the answer to your every problem which is destroying your life.

Accepting the point of his close friend, Leo moved to the monastery where the Zen master with profound knowledge and wisdom had been residing with serenity. The path to the monastery was not easy. Leo had to face a number of difficulties to get the answers to his problems. When Leo and his friend reached the monastery, they saw some people coming out of the monastery. Leo humbly asked them to stop for a while and inquired about the Zen master.

Those few people told Leo that the Zen master's teachings and wisdom were beyond any description. "If you have come here, then you will not return empty handed" they told Leo. Thereafter, Leo approached the Zen master. After hearing the immeasurable pain deep inside Leo's heart, the Zen master said to Leo:

> "My child, in this world no one wants to live
> and stay with anyone who remains sad, worried
> and unhappy because everyone thinks this type of
> individual being as ill fated. If you really want
> to attract people and draw their attention towards
> yourself, then you have to be happy and cheerful
> not only from inside, but from outside too. Leo,
> always remember that we get what we focus on. If we
> focus on problems and worries, then we get the same
> in our life, but if we focus on the solutions to
> those problems and worries, then we start getting

solutions to them. It is very important for us on
what we are focusing on our life, we must embrace
it, in this case focusing on joy, happiness, freedom
and peace. You never have to let people know that
you are broken from the inside because in this world
the number of good hearted and sympathetic people
are less as compared to the people who make fun of
our bad situations. Leo my child, in this world,
people give less support and more betrayal. Never
let people know about your problems, otherwise no
one will stay with you for long. The root cause
for all your problems is worrying and overthinking.
That's why I'm going to tell you four ways with the
help of which you will surely kick out the habit of
unnecessary worrying and overthinking.

After this, the Zen master starts telling the four important ways to
get out of the tornado of overthinking and worrying. The Zen master
imparted the four ways/waves by saying:

ONE – Never carry the burden of unwanted, negative and
unnecessary thoughts. They will never benefit you in any way but
they will always have the power to destroy your peace of mind and
soul. Just live freely, focus on what you can change and what's in
your hands. Don't focus on what you cannot change. If you ever try
to change something that is not your cup of tea, you will get nothing
but hopelessness and disappointment and this creates worry and
anxiety.

TWO – Never argue with anyone. Argument with any fool may lead
your inner peace to uneasiness and this will ultimately make you
worried. When we argue with a fool it is our loss because at that time
we are trying to explain our point to a person who does not know
how to understand. In his eyes, only his words are right and the
words of others are wrong. If you are able to stay positive in negative
situations, that's where you start winning in your life. Why disturb
your peace of mind by talking to such a foolish person? **Silence is
the best answer from a wise man to a fool**. In this way we can save
ourselves from worrying unnecessarily.

After telling two noble ways to avoid worrying unnecessarily, the Zen
master paused for a while. After that the Zen master told Leo the
third way and said:

THREE – You know how many such negative and unwanted thoughts always go in our mind which push us into the depths of despair. We can free ourselves from its web through meditation. Through meditation we can stop the tempest of all kinds of thoughts arising inside our mind and can create a new space for new and positive thoughts and ideas. So that we can live our life without worries. Meditation not only changes us from the inside but it helps us to look good from the outside also. Meditation brings a positive change in our way of thinking and with this our day passes peacefully.

FOUR – If you want to live a life free from worries, anxieties and problems, then always speak less and speak only when it is necessary, and if possible, then whenever you speak, speak useful. If you keep talking excessively anywhere, then people will start ignoring you and will not respect you and your words and will call you a fool. Speak only when it is necessary to speak. First think 10 times, then speak. Many times, because of your excessive speaking unknowingly something comes out of your mouth which should not have come out and then about which we keep repenting again and again and then we end up becoming a victim of deep anxiety and worry.

Remember one thing, when you speak at the right time after thoughtfully speaking when needed, then people will have to listen to your words carefully. This habit will not improve quickly but will definitely improve with regular effort. The habit of thoughtfully speaking will undoubtedly save yourself from unnecessary troubles and worries.

After saying this, the Zen master became silent and calms down and starts his meditation once again because the master had told Leo all the four best ways to avoid unnecessary worrying and overthinking. Leo had understood that the master had said his final words. He gets up and thanks the master for imparting him these four valuable lessons. Now Leo bowed respectfully before the master and returned to his village.

The people of his village observed some small but life changing behavior in Leo since his return from the Zen monastery. The villagers noticed that Leo was no longer worried unnecessarily for anything. He was no longer a man lost in deep thought as he used to be. He was now happy and wherever he goes he spreads happiness and peace. Everyone now began to enjoy his company. In this way, with the help of the wisdom of the Zen master, Leo had changed his life completely.

We can also cultivate a core mindset where there is no room for worries and overthinking. Just by putting everything aside, which makes us worried, anxious and unhappy, don't focus on worries, focus on the solution to them and then see how big changes will appear in your life. Life doesn't have to be difficult. Your perception of anything is what makes it difficult. Live in the present, whatever it is that you do, do it with love. Treat anything as an activity for your body, mind and soul and not as a job. Do things for enjoyment.

> NOW IS THE TIME. THERE IS ONLY "NOW". PAST MOMENTS AND FUTURE MOMENTS ARE SIMPLY PREVIOUS "NOWS" AND FUTURE "NOWS".

BLESSING

29 Goodwill towards others. The wellspring of generosity and graciousness. A blessing from yourself is a well-timed gift to the right person at the right time serendipitously. Manifestation requires attunement to the individual or idea for potency. But you can also put good things out there and trust the universe to share them with the right people. The universe will help you. You just need to conceptualize a great good and share it somehow. But if you cannot conceptualize a great good, there's many to pick from that are tried and true with the sociological buoyancy to be floated and received easily with potency depending on the attunement of both parties (you and whoever or whatever it is that you focus on attracting/getgetting/manifesting). And a word of advice, it's a bad idea to float too many blessings towards one individual and it's more beneficial to be generally benevolent and generous to everyone who enters your life rather than specific people who are important to you. If you do this then you will be blessed wherever you go.

A blessing is an event manifested when a conscious and a subconscious mind align.

QUESTION - Does it mean that we can manifest within minutes or hours if conscious and subconscious align?

ANSWER - The subconscious doesn't follow our time schedules. Rule of thumb is 21 days for a rewiring of beliefs.

When you receive a blessing you shall share it with others. Otherwise, it can turn into a curse. Many billionaires know how the manifestation works that's why they give lots of money to charities. Many of these charities are run by billionaires, politicians, but under fake names. But you must do good to receive good. The energy you put out, comes back to you. It is reciprocity.

Your intentions with the "blessing" have a lot to do with what they receive which has to be from true intention and backed up by a strong emotion. The person that receives this blessing also has to be willing to take in this energy that you are bringing, if they don't know or if they are in a bad head space the "blessing" will have no effect because once you put your intentions out there its on them to take the good energy in. Lots of times our loved ones feel like maybe they deserve what's going on and its really hard for them or us to accept what life throws at us but we are the cause. Life will throw back at us based on what we emit externally through our words and actions which will cause a reaction in the quantum field/aether/universe.

Anything a person focuses on expands. Relationships build and attract new situations. Every fine reason is blessing. Every divine reason is why virtues are described with individual names. A statement given to the universe and it responds to your wishes and desires.

What we think, we say.
What we say, we hear.
What we hear, we take to heart.
What we take to heart, will manifest in our reality around us.
What we put into our minds we think.

A real blessing is when a self realized person gives you a blessing and in turn speeds up your own spiritual evolution.

Are all timeliness (current one and all other potentialities) running simultaneously? It is our vibrational alignment with what we want/desire that determines our alignment with a given timeline. For example, if you think, say and behave positively, then you will attract a timeline of people and circumstances that will benefit you and the world. The same applies if you think and act negatively, you will attract a negative timeline or reality which you will struggle and suffer. Never forget that you are both the cause and the effect. Practice gratitude, instead of being ego driven, closed off , judgment and reactive.

Gratitude will open you up to blessing. It will open you up to the potential beauty and abundance possible with just a shift in perspective. Just about any given physical or nonphysical experience is for you to experience in their own full potential. You are an alchemist. The tools have been given to you, the tools are your body, your mind and your emotions. How your express yourself is how good you use the tools. Energy is always in motion, you must flow with it. Everything that you do you must do it with love, without expecting anything in return.

WHATEVER YOU DO. DO IT WITH LOVE. AS LONG
AS WHATEVER YOU DO. DERIVES FROM A
GENUINE LOVING AND CARING INTENTION.

ARE YOU AN EXTRA-TERRESTRIAL?

30 Terra means land in Latin. Extra Terra means extra land. Extra terrestrial=Beings from beyond the Antarctic circle or wall, or from the inner Earth.
Below you'll read a page from the book *I AM THE KEY THAT OPENS ALL DOORS* by Saimir Kercanaj.

"Whether you are a human or an extra-terrestrial, depends on how you picture your reality. If you think you are a human, then it means that you have lost your spirituality and you must strive for obtaining it. To obtain it, you must stop being a human. What does "must stop being a human" mean? Well, it is not that you will die, or disappear in thin air or something. It is all about your consciousness. It is about expanding it beyond what you have lived your life so far. You must not be driven by Earthly redundancy.

Do not be driven by materialism, sex, power etc. You must have a higher purpose for existing. And if you are an E.T., then you are a spiritual force in the Universe that is channelling itself through your human embodiment to serve the planet and its course of evolution in the consciousness ladder. You decide whether you are a human body, or whether you are a spirit dressed in a meaty flesh/physical body. The Universe rearranges itself to serve your picture of reality. What you strive to be, the Universe will make sure to serve you. It is how it works. If things that you desire do not get accomplished, it is because you have not innerstood yet what you are.

The Universe/Creator is your servant in the sense that because you are created from Love, you have been given free will which is 'Love'. Someone that loves you, will let you choose freely without constraints, right? Why do you think that extra-terrestrial in movies or fake news are mostly portrayed as ugly/mean creatures? That's because those that control the content of the movies, do not want you to realize who you really are. "As you believe so shall it be" is a powerful Universal law which dictates that what you beLIEve, becomes your reality. Don't you think that it is time to question your beliefs about the Extra-terrestrials? What are you, a human being or an Extra-terrestrial? Your answer will determine your destination.

Your answer will determine whether you will move up higher in the consciousness/reality ladder or whether you will stay where you are (for now). The only major problem that can slow you down to expand your consciousness is whether you believe in reincarnation or not. If you don't believe in reincarnation, then clearly you are a human being, but if you believe in reincarnation, then definitely you are a spiritual person and will progress much, much faster than those that believe that life is only birth and death (one life and that's it). Know that on the 4th dimension you are Christ Consciousness being. You came here to bring your love, light and wisdom to assist the planet in its transition from 3d to 5D. You have just forgotten. But you will remember it, guaranteed. I strongly suggest you write down your dreams and any particular situation that happens in your everyday life. They are messages. Even if they may not seem important, write them down anyway, they will be useful at the right time, at the right place.

There have always been Extra-terrestrials on Earth. A big influx has happened in recent decades. They have lent their consciousness to Earthly humans to assist in the transition."

Everything is energy, what you are doesn't matter, as long as you know what you are. Everything springs from the same source. Separation is the greatest illusion. You are a combination of countless illusions. What is true is what you make it out to be, what or who you are is determined by you. The sooner you begin to not be attached to names, ideas, nationalities, social status etc., the sooner you will become free. What you think you are is a limitation. What you are is **F R E E D O M**. Freedom doesn't really mean that you can do whatever you want without inflicting any consequences on yourself. Freedom means that whatever you do, you do it by being your own authority and whatever you do, contributes to the betterment of yourself, your loved ones and the world. Just as other beings are extraterrestrials to you, so are you an extraterrestrial to them. Just as a German is a human to a Mexican so a Mexican is a human to a German. The difference lies in what people have been conditioned to label others as.

Question: Where are you from?
Answer: It is not a country.

It is up to you, you are from wherever you believe yourself to be from. The answer is in you, you create your own reality. But in the end whatever it is that you create, you will continue seeking the ultimate truth by creating in accordance with the law of love and not with the absence of it.

> YOU ARE FROM THE SAME PRIMORDIAL SOURCE AS EVERYONE ELSE KNOWN OR UNKNOWN TO YOU.

CELEBRATING YOUR BIRTHDAY
IS A DARK RITUAL

31 First of all, you were born incomplete. The umbilical cord that connected you with your mother was prematurely cut, making you an invalid. When the cord is prematurely cut, you get much less oxygen, nutrients and stem cells. That's why many times they have to hold the newborn upside down and slap the butt cheeks so that the system gets a shock/oxygen. Just like when an adult's heart stops and the doctors use a defibrillator to deliver a therapeutic shock. In the case of the newborn, besides the intentional mistake to prematurely cut the umbilical cord as opposed to letting it fall by itself in 2-3 days, the other mistake in delivering babies is having the women lie down.

That is wrong, the best way to deliver a baby is in water, either in delivery centers where they have pools of water for this purpose or even in a bathtub. Of course, as a mother you are scared that something might happen to the child but first arm yourself with knowledge, look for a midwife and go from there. The mainstream hospitals/maternities are dark ritual live cemeteries. Most people think that death is when your physical body stops existing. That kind of death is the last of your worries. You should be more concerned with living as a walking dead. Why do we say '**rest in peace**' when someone passes away? Why don't we also say, '**LIVE IN PEACE**'? Apparently there is an imbalance in one's life. Death and life are both sides of the same coin.

None can do without the other. Every day of your life you are alive and breathing, and yet death has crossed your mind many times. So, are you really living or are you pretending you are living? Also consider that this economical, materialistic, hard-working system is created from everyone's birth certificate and it is obvious that we all began our life as a zombie that needs permission to get married, to purchase a house, land, to work (to be hired they need your STRAWMAN's fictional man-made legal documents).

Does that make sense to need paper documents to live? There is a theory that the *fallen angels** a.k.a the Anunnaki created this "birthday celebration" as a dark ritual to keep the population under control and to keep people from living for hundreds or thousands of years of age. Since it is proven beyond a doubt that thoughts/words create reality, every time you say or think about your age, your internal main switch is telling/conditioning your billions or trillions of cells to age. The candle represents your life years. The cake represents the placenta that was unjustly taken away from your mother and left you dead at sea. Below I mention a book about the STRAWMAN.

There you will read about "dead at sea" of what it means as it is related to the MARITIME law of the sea a.k.a. the law of the pirates. That's what those in unjust power are, pirates that steal and kill human populations for personal gain. That's too big of a subject for me to explain here. Every time you blow the candles you are blowing your life away, the years that past, as if they never existed.

*fallen angels** - metaphorically we are also the fallen angels, since we fell in the lower mind, we lost connection with the Source. We disconnected from the higher mind.

For a more robust explanation of how we came to be and how the birthday certificate was deviously created I highly suggest you read the book *"YOU ARE NOT A STRAWMAN YOU ARE THE ZYGOTE"* by Saimir X. Kercanaj. I was purchasing some stuff on Amazon and I stumbled upon this book about the STRAWMAN. I had heard about the STRAWMAN subject but never looked into it, so I purchased it, read it and boy I was shocked at how deviously we have been dupped/deceived by those that have no interest in us awakening. You know what? I'm going to insert below a short excerpt from that book.

When the baby first comes out of the womb, he is still connected to the umbilical cord. So now you have this straddle, this biological straddle. The baby is at the point of entry into the new world, in full view of everyone in the present moment. Then the umbilical cord straddling the two worlds going back into the womb, going back to the wall of the uterus where the rest of the baby is attached in most cases.

Now you have the baby in the present, the straddle through the umbilical cord back into the old world, the water-based world of mother and you have the rest of the baby still in that unseen realm, still not been witnessed yet. When they clamp and cut the cord, they actually create a duality. So, baby's out here now, disconnected from his origin, biologically and physically disconnected. And everyone is like "Oh, look at the beautiful baby boy/or girl" But what about of the rest of the baby? Almost everyone didn't know about this abandonment of the rest of the baby that was left behind in the womb.

This is an incomplete delivery. Go to webster's online and look up the medical definition of the word delivery. You will see that it says: A fetus and its membranes is a delivery. When they don't deliver the membranes (placenta plus uncut umbilical cord), that's not a delivery at all. That's an ABORTION. The moment they cut the umbilical cord; they create an abortion. But you don't think of it as an abortion because you see the baby alive and well, unknown to you that the baby is considered already dead/abandoned (since umbilical cord and placenta was left behind) by the legal authorities.

*Also, you don't think it is an abortion because to you an abortion is associated with the initial stage of pregnancy when abortion/ miscarriages happen. The abortion is what creates the birth certificate. More like "**death certificate.**"*

Look at the word "birthday", it has the word DAY in it. It is for the day that you were born. Even if you wanted to celebrate a birthday, that would not be the end of the world if you only celebrated the day that someone is born, on that day alone. It is madness to celebrate each year. Each year you are cursing that person but also cursing yourself through the law of manifesting your thoughts. I used to frequent a lot of social media and I was conversing a lot with many people about many subjects. About many of the subjects, some of them would ridicule me, or straight deny. Years later some of those people are talking/teaching about the very same things they were opposed to. The point is that if this birthday subject seems ridiculous to you, I suggest you consider the possibility that there may be some truth to it. If you think to live up to 80 or 90 years of age is normal, that is a reality that you have created in your mind because you have been conditioned to not think otherwise.

The mind gets tricked by numbers. When you think about the number of your age, your mind accesses the subconscious part of it or the hard disc drive HDD. What is in your subconscious? Habits live there. So, if you have wished a '*happy birthday*' every year to many people and thought also about your own birthday, then you have trained your psyche/biological self to self-destruct. Don't do things because others do it. You get lost if you follow the herd. Find your own way.

"Finding your way" means to get away from the multitudes. Only then you will be able to hear the whispers of your own real voice, instead of replaying corrupted scenarios as a result of countless opinions from others that do not know themselves, let alone knowing you. Every day is worth it to celebrate your existence. The past is gone, the future hasn't arrived yet. You can only exist and live in the **PRESENT**.

PRE-SENT means - *sending in advance.*

With every negative or positive thought, word or action of the present you are sending a signal (planting a seed) for the future. So be careful of your thoughts, words, and behavior.

> THOUGHTS ARE POWERFUL. THOUGHTS ARE
> DOUBLE EDGED SWORDS. YOU CAN BUILD OR
> DESTROY WITH YOUR THOUGHTS.

THE TRUE NEW YEAR

32 The beginning of the New Year is not on the 1st of January but on MARCH 21st or whenever the Sun enters Aries. When the Sun enters Aries, this is when flowers bloom, in the spring. This symbolizes the beginning of new life. Passover is celebrated by the Jews, they eat lamb because the Sun has passed/crossed over the winter and Aries, the lamb. Christians celebrate Easter which is the resurrection of Jesus. Jesus or Yashua (the name does not matter) is the son/Son. He has 12 disciples representing the 12 zodiac signs. If you haven't already seen the famous painting "the last supper" by Leonardo Da Vinci (*check the image on the next page*), it is a painting of Jesus and his 12 disciples, four groups (Gospels-seasons) of three disciples representing the 12 months, four seasons. They changed the New Year to be in Capricorn because they wanted us to not be in rhythm with nature.

The Sun/Son (Jesus metaphorically) is the light of the world. The fake new year falls in Capricorn where everything is dead/winter which then created April fool's which is the real NEW YEAR. Astronomy and astrology were studied by Egyptians, Greeks and Ethiopians who existed even before Jews or the Roman Catholics. They follow the original calendar before it was changed A.D. Do not get stuck on dates. Many dates, places or names have been altered, butchered and mistranslated. Simply ask this common sense question: *When is nature mostly alive, in the spring/summer or fall/winter?*

There are solar and lunar years. Nature's cycles are more fitting for humans because we are indeed nature. Winter is the depth of darkness for the Northern hemisphere. We must winter as the animals do and not set goals and create havoc to our system by taking actions that prohibits the seed from growing. Darkness is ripe for sowing seeds, just as when you sow vegetable seeds in the soil (in darkness). Just like animals so must we plant the seed in the dark/winter by staying calm and not spending much energy. Also, in the winter we must eat much less because naturally the body is in a sort of hibernation mode. We must be in parallel with nature.

"The last supper"

*I have seen people argue whether this (the above image) is the **Last Supper, Dyonisus' feast** or **Thoth's dinner** (I made up this last one:). Does it really matter? What matters is the message. For as long as people keep arguing/fighting over names and other redundancy by being distracted, the so called slave masters will keep controlling public opinion.*

Observe what nature does and mimic it. Regardless of which day/number on any calendar in the world that you may use, what matters is that in your mind, you must realize that something new is something alive and not dead. There are all sorts of calendars out there, African, Vedic calendar etc. Some are more accurate than others, as far as the Gregorian calendar goes but the most accurate calendar if up there in the sky.

The old Bibles had more truths than the King James versions. But no matter how many books you read; your common sense is more important. And I mean common sense when you are not tainted by external butchered information. Simply connect with nature/self and the truth will appear, without you having to look for it. Never forget to connect with the child within, don't lose your ROSEBUD. You'll read soon enough about the rosebud.

WHAT IS APRIL FOOLS DAY?
In medieval France, New Year was celebrated on April 1st. Then in 1562 (or 562 based on the 1000 years they added on the calendar

out of thin year), Pope Gregory introduced a new calendar for the Christian world, changing the New Year from April 1st to January 1st. With no modern communications (as far as **fabricated his-story** goes), news traveled slowly and new ideas were often questioned. Well, at least back in the day they questioned authority, not like in the modern times where people go along with what the government says.

Many people did not hear of this change and others chose to ignore it. These people were called "fools". Invitations to non-existent 'New Year' parties were sent and other practical jokes were played. Over time this evolved into a tradition on playing pranks on the 1st of April each year. Did this evolve naturally or was there a hidden hand that conditioned people to make fun and be distracted from the real truth, that instead of making fun of each other people should celebrate the spring, the beginning. Having in mind that there have been many different calendars throughout time.

The real new year should begin when the Sun enters Aries, regardless of what the date on a piece of paper says. Most of us think that we are in 2024 (at the time of this writing) but are we in 2024? Did they perhaps add 1000 years on the Gregorian calendar to make it seem like the amazing old Tartarian and other civilizations structures all over the world were build by ancients as opposed to only a few centuries ago?

Did the dark ages really exist? You may say "Yes, I read it from a book, or that you learned it in school". Question everything, including the information in this book. Reading and researching is useful so that you are faced with all sorts of information. Then you should criss cross information and form an educated opinion. The only absolute truth is what you personally experience.

DON'T LOSE YOUR ROSE BUD
In the 1941 movie "**Citizen Kane**" "ROSEBUD" is the last word spoken by the protagonist Charles Kane on his deathbed at the beginning of the movie. This word was a mystery for most of the movie's duration until the end where "Rosebud" is eventually revealed to be the name of Kane's beloved sled from his childhood. For all of his adulthood he was unhappy, but "Rosebud" alludes to the last time Kane was truly happy, when he was a child where money didn't mean anything to him or any other child for that matter.

Sometimes when I go to the mall with my husband and my children, I jump and play like a child. I feel alive. Quite a few people look at me like I'm crazy. Because they have been molded in a hive mind mentality where you have to behave a certain way, based on societal norms. But I did not harm anyone, actually I made others laugh and smile. Even though they would not act like me (not right away anyway), deep down they knew/know that being a child means happiness, means no worries and no fears.

Of course, by being an adult it means that there are responsibilities, but where is the limit of responsibilities? There is a big difference between moral responsibility or responsibility to be a man-made law-abiding citizen [citizen=employee of the state a.k.a. slave) that serves the corporations that want you to spill your blood and energy to feed their multibillion-dollar businesses. The title of this subchapter means to not lose the child within. A child is curious of the world, but also naïve and reckless.

```
Combine the curiosity and innocence of the child
with common sense and critical thinking of an adult
so that you can be a complete being, otherwise
you'll just remain a naive and reckless child in a
grown up body.
```

Unless you grow up you will treat others as your parents when you were a child, needing their attention.

GROW UP. BE A LEADER OF YOUR THOUGHTS DONT
LET DISTORTED THOUGHTS CAUSE YOU TO SAY AND
DO SOMETHING THAT YOU WILL REGRET.

EVERYTHING IS INTERCONNECTED

33 No matter what everyone says, everyone talks about the same thing but from a different angle or point of view which is based on one's level of awareness. Picture yourself on the ground in front of a 15 story building holding an object of 30cm/12-inch of diameter. On each floor there is a person holding in their hand the same object and size as you. From your point of view the object on each floor is of a different size, even to the people from each floor holding the object, to each other the object seems to be of a different size. Everyone insists that the object is 30 cm/12-inch, but the object is different for each person's point of view.

All the people are holding the same sized object. Just as you and everyone else are talking about the same thing but from a different perspective. To confirm that the people above or below have the same size object, you will have to climb up or down the stairs. The same applies about knowledge. If you want to resonate with those above you, you must open your mind that perhaps their object's size is indeed what they are telling you. If you do not open your mind you will hold on to your belief and you will not be able to climb higher in the ladder of knowledge.

You might keep arguing and defending your belief that their object is not the same size as yours. Everyone is right from their own perspective. Everyone of us is the ONE. All of us make the GREAT ONE that holds everything together. You are the one and everyone at the same time.

Look at the disco ball. It has squares of different color hues (this book is in black and white though), there is white, black, grey and a combination of these three. See each of these little squares as the perspective of one person. Some squares (*perspectives*) are blurry (*confused people*), some are dark (*hurting people and animals and nature*), some are clear (*self-aware critical thinking*) and some are very bright (*love and light confused people thinking they are above anyone else*). All these squares form the whole object. Just as all the perceptions of all the people form the WHOLE reality with each person living their own little reality.

In your head you have a version of everyone else and that version is only yours. The same applies for each individual from their perspective. Even though it may seem we are separate from each other, we are each other. Even though it may seem we are connected to each other, we are separated from each other, since everything and everyone outside of us is a creation in our mind. The intricacy and the convoluted nature of creation is so amazing.

> The heaven is present at all times, it is just a matter of tuning to it. Heaven is a frequency and not a place. You can go somewhere in nature where you love it so much that you can call it "heaven" if you want. But I am talking about the heaven which is present in every step that you take where you operate from the heart and from a critical thinking mindset. To create a beautiful and happy life you must think for yourself, you must be empathetic toward all sentient beings and then watch how you will attune to that universal love frequency.

You are the single point which the whole universe revolves around in your reality. Only you can create your reality, everyone else's reality is their own. You are an NPC in other people's reality. Project from within, from the center of your being. In your own reality you are the chosen one, just as everyone else is the chosen in their own reality. Ask the innocent child (not the wounded one) within:

What do you want to be when you grow up?

And the answer will always be: **FREE**

<u>YOU ARE THE ONE</u>

Will you take a moment of your time and do your part in reviewing this book, so that it can help it be exposed to more people? Humanity needs to be free and it deserves peace. Only those that arm themselves with knowledge can be free. Spread the word...

Sacrifice a few moments of your time
and review this book on **AMAZON**.

Truth appreciates you.

MY THOUGHTS ON REVIEWING BOOKS OR ANYTHING ELSE ON AMAZON

I read halfway through a fictional book that had a good message about truth and I couldn't finish it. The book was great but it was written in a fictional format and I do not really like fictional books, but this book had underlying truths in it. There was nothing wrong with the book. It was me who was expecting a non-fictional read. Regardless, I learned a few things from the book. There is another book called "The Alchemist" by Paulo Coelho, this too is a fictional book about a boy searching for a treasure. But it is all a metaphorical story about the treasure being hidden within us all. And I loved this book. I suggest you read books to understand and not for the sake of some kind of challenge that many do, such as: *"I challenge myself to read 40-50 books this year"*.

Even if you read thousands of books, it doesn't mean anything. Your perception of who you are and what life is about, can change just by one or two books alone, without having to read many. You do not have to read a book in its entirety if it's not interesting. A book may be interesting to you but not to someone else and vice versa. A book is like a person, would you deny a sibling, parent or a friend just because you don't agree with something they said? The words you are reading may be 2D characters but the words are written by a sentient being like you. In my opinion, the reason why you like or dislike a book or anything that you purchase is because of at least two factors:

1... Expectations.

Psychologically we human beings feel good when what we read, resonates with us, but what doesn't resonate, we tend to ridicule or deny the possibility that what we read could hold some truths to it. You must always consider anything that doesn't align with your expectations may be true. And what aligns, may not be so. You are energy and energy has different levels. Energy is always present at all times. It is all electromagnetism. When something resonates with you, it means that both energies, yours and what you read, are magnetized toward each other.

But it doesn't mean that it is the truth. There are people that love soap operas, movies where those movies/shows are full of betrayal, jealousy, cheating etc. As an example, if you were ever cheated on by someone and then held a grudge, you will resonate with the hatred of someone in the TV show that was cheated on. In this case you resonate with the actor's emotions.

Grudge or hate is a low vibrational frequency. So, what I do is treat every book as if it is fiction. This way I do not get disappointed anymore. I find truths in all books. Since you change constantly, what you previously thought was not true, may turn out to be true at a later date when you achieve a better understanding of life and yourself.

2... PERSONAL LANGUAGE CAPACITY/UNDERSTANDING

Different people have a specific capacity of how many words they know. Plus, the same words that most people use, are interpreted differently by many. One example is the word "judging". Many people see this word as a negative one. That's because it is related to the previous point "EXPECTATION". When you speak your mind when talking to someone, if what you say is not to their liking, they say that you are judgemental. And if you satisfy their ego, then you are a nice person and they will like you. Always speak your mind. Better to be disliked for freely expressing yourself, rather then be liked for pleasing someone else's expectation.

The word "*judging*" means to judge right from wrong. Even though everyone must realize what is right from wrong through their own moral compass, they should not be triggered in a bad way by your words. If they do, then they put more power to your words than on theirs. I like to analyze human mind/behavior so sometimes I check reviews on many products but for the sake of this subject I'll talk about reviews on books. One reviewer wrote in a book (that I read a while back) that the information in the book was not true. That reviewer was a religious person. Now, as someone who thinks for her self I ask:

If she thought the information was not true, then she must have known what was true. And if she knew what the truth was, then why did she purchase/read the book? I'll tell you why, it's because deep inside of her, she knew that what she was taught (by religion) didn't resonate with her soul/spirit. So, deep inside her she was in search for answers, hence reading books. When you read books that shine light on religious lies, ego kicks in and tries to defend anyone that threatens one's beliefs.

What I end up saying is to have an open mind that truth is everywhere. If you do not agree or believe something, it doesn't make it a lie. If you believe it, it doesn't make it true either. Throughout your (and anyone else's) life, truths and lies exchange places many times. What does this mean? It means that what you think is true or a lie is in direct proportion with your current level of knowledge at any given time.

Some things that I wrote in this book I considered them to be lies a few years ago, and some others I thought were true. Always have an open mind that what you disagree with, may hold some truth to it. If I were to say that humans have 7 fingers on each hand you would outright deny it, as would I. This is not what I'm talking about. I am talking about anything that is outside of you.

If I say that:

> The grass is blue and that walking on the grass (grounding) is very important for your positive (pollution) ions to be discharged in the grass and you will receive the negative (healing) ions from the Earth (soil, grass) through the bottom of your feet, will you dismiss the important knowledge just because you don't agree with the grass being blue?

The truth is everywhere, including within the darkness and in plain sight.

Thank you for reading.

In the next page check a list of books that you might find interesting. Never judge a book by its cover.

Resources/Bibliography

I AM THE KEY THAT OPENS ALL DOORS by Saimir Kercanaj

REGENERATION CALENDAR by Kelly-Marie Kerr

SAMADHI by Ivan Antic

GAIN WISDOM THROUGH PRACTICED KNOWLEDGE by Rimias K. Neo

Natural Treasure – Quest for Knowledge, health & Freedom by Blake Cyrier

BODY MIND SOUL by Saimir Kercanaj

CULTIVATING STILLNESS by Eva Wong

SEX AND REPRESSION IN SAVAGE SOCIETY by Bronislaw Malinowski

LIMITLESS POTENTIAL by Saimir Kercanaj

THE TAO OF HEALTH, SEX AND LONGEVITY by Daniel P. Reid

THIRD EYE AWAKENING by Ella Hughes

THE ART OF SEEING by Nathaniel

THE REPTILIAN ALIEN ORIGINS OF THE HUMAN SPECIES by AKTAR: Pleiadian Light Warrior
REBUILD YOURSELF FROM WITHIN by J.J. and Tamo

Books on the "STRAWMAN" subject.

YOU ARE NOT A STRAWMAN YOU ARE THE ZYGOTE by Saimir X. Kercanaj
MEET YOUR STRAWMAN AND WHATEVER YOU WANT TO KNOW by David E. Robinson

YouTube

Kundalini booster by Kelly-Marie Kerr
https://www.youtube.com/watch?v=HJU8SVyvEto

How to activate your third eye / Kundalini by Video Advice
https://www.youtube.com/watch?v=QdzT5TKDl4o

ACKNOWLEDGEMENT

A big appreciation to the authors mentioned in this book and all those that are putting an effort in transmuting themselves to greatness. Everyone that I have met in my life had something to teach me. Learning never ends. Knowledge is unlimited.

I thank my husband and children for being patient with me. Peace,freedom and prosperity is everyone's right. Together we are stronger.

TOGETHER WE ARE ONE.

<u>NOTES</u>

<u>NOTES</u>

<u>NOTES</u>

<u>NOTES</u>

Printed in Dunstable, United Kingdom